Current CONTROVERSIES

Alternative Therapies

Sylvia Engdahl, Book Editor

GREENHAVEN PRESS
A part of Gale, Cengage Learning

GALE
CENGAGE Learning·

Detroit • New York • San Francisco • New Haven, Conn • Waterville, Maine • London

GALE
CENGAGE Learning·

Elizabeth Des Chenes, *Managing Editor*

© 2012 Greenhaven Press, a part of Gale, Cengage Learning

Gale and Greenhaven Press are registered trademarks used herein under license.

For more information, contact:
Greenhaven Press
27500 Drake Rd.
Farmington Hills, MI 48331-3535
Or you can visit our Internet site at gale.cengage.com

For product information and technology assistance, contact us at

Gale Customer Support, 1-800-877-4253
For permission to use material from this text or product, submit all requests online at www.cengage.com/permissions

Further permissions questions can be emailed to permissionrequest@cengage.com

Articles in Greenhaven Press anthologies are often edited for length to meet page requirements. In addition, original titles of these works are changed to clearly present the main thesis and to explicitly indicate the author's opinion. Every effort is made to ensure that Greenhaven Press accurately reflects the original intent of the authors. Every effort has been made to trace the owners of copyrighted material.

Cover image copyright © Paul Prescott/Shutterstock.com.

LIBRARY OF CONGRESS CATALOGING-IN-PUBLICATION DATA

Alternative therapies / Sylvia Engdahl, book editor.
    p. cm. -- (Current controversies) Summary: "Alternative Therapies: Is the Growing Use of Complementary and Alternative Therapies Beneficial?; Are the Major Alternatives to Conventional Medicine Safe and Effective?; Should the Government Restrict the Use of Alternative Therapies?; What Complementary Therapies Are Used Along with Conventional Medicine?"-- Provided by publisher.
    Includes bibliographical references and index.
    ISBN 978-0-7377-5610-4 (hardback) -- ISBN 978-0-7377-5611-1 (paperback)
    1. Alternative medicine. 2. Naturopathy. I. Engdahl, Sylvia.
    R733.A5157 2011
    615.5'35--dc23
                                                            2011024601

Printed in the United States of America
2 3 4 5 6   16 15 14 13 12

FD172

Contents

Chapter 1: Is the Growing Use of Complementary and Alternative Therapies Beneficial?

Yes: Complementary and Alternative Therapies Serve Needs Not Met by Conventional Medicine

Alternative therapies help people feel better, even if such therapies are worthless in the scientific sense. They should be regarded as spiritual practices with psychological healing benefits, whereas conventional medicine cures disease without necessarily improving the patient's subjective feelings. Both healing and curing are important, but they cannot and should not be integrated.

No: Most Complementary and Alternative Therapies Are Unproven and Sometimes Harmful

Chapter 2: Are the Major Alternatives to Conventional Medicine Safe and Effective?

Chiropractors are now serving as primary health care providers and are covered by many insurance plans. Most treat mainly back and neck pain and often succeed in reducing it, though the claim of others that manipulating the spine can cure all kinds of illness is more controversial. Millions of patients choose chiropractic care and believe that they are helped by it.

Naturopathy's goal is to remove the barriers to self-healing and to eliminate the cause of illness rather than suppress the symptoms. It uses low-risk, natural treatments and customizes advice to individual patients, treating the whole person, not merely the disease.

Robert T. Carroll

Naturopathy is based on the belief that the body can heal itself and offers allegedly natural remedies intended to help it do so, especially for enhancing the immune system. Yet there is no evidence that most disease is caused by faulty immune systems.

Chapter 3: Should the Government Restrict the Use of Alternative Therapies?

Yes: The Government Should Favor Conventional Medicine and Judge Alternatives by Its Standards

Brennen McKenzie

Americans are divided in their opinions about who should decide what medical therapies are acceptable. The health freedom lobby argues that consumers and market forces alone should regulate them, but advocates of science-based medicine consider it self-evident that it is the role of government to do so. Court decisions have affirmed the government's power in this regard.

Steven Novella

Competent adults have a constitutional right to refuse medical treatment, but the government should protect minors from unconventional beliefs by forcing them to receive whatever treatment it deems necessary to save their lives.

Most alternative therapies are not covered by Medicare or other insurance. People who use them in place of conventional medicine are accustomed to having to pay for them, but with the new law they will also have to pay for standard medical insurance that they do not use, so they may no longer be able to afford health care they find acceptable.

Tai chi is a form of low-impact exercise that began in China as a martial art but today is popular all over the world for its effect on health. It involves slow, controlled body movements that improve muscle tone, circulation, flexibility, and balance, among other benefits, making it especially suitable for older people and those recovering from illness.

Foreword

By definition, controversies are "discussions of questions in which opposing opinions clash" (Webster's Twentieth Century Dictionary Unabridged). Few would deny that controversies are a pervasive part of the human condition and exist on virtually every level of human enterprise. Controversies transpire between individuals and among groups, within nations and between nations. Controversies supply the grist necessary for progress by providing challenges and challengers to the status quo. They also create atmospheres where strife and warfare can flourish. A world without controversies would be a peaceful world; but it also would be, by and large, static and prosaic.

The Series' Purpose

The purpose of the Current Controversies series is to explore many of the social, political, and economic controversies dominating the national and international scenes today. Titles selected for inclusion in the series are highly focused and specific. For example, from the larger category of criminal justice, Current Controversies deals with specific topics such as police brutality, gun control, white collar crime, and others. The debates in Current Controversies also are presented in a useful, timeless fashion. Articles and book excerpts included in each title are selected if they contribute valuable, long-range ideas to the overall debate. And wherever possible, current information is enhanced with historical documents and other relevant materials. Thus, while individual titles are current in focus, every effort is made to ensure that they will not become quickly outdated. Books in the Current Controversies series will remain important resources for librarians, teachers, and students for many years.

In addition to keeping the titles focused and specific, great care is taken in the editorial format of each book in the series. Book introductions and chapter prefaces are offered to provide background material for readers. Chapters are organized around several key questions that are answered with diverse opinions representing all points on the political spectrum. Materials in each chapter include opinions in which authors clearly disagree as well as alternative opinions in which authors may agree on a broader issue but disagree on the possible solutions. In this way, the content of each volume in Current Controversies mirrors the mosaic of opinions encountered in society. Readers will quickly realize that there are many viable answers to these complex issues. By questioning each author's conclusions, students and casual readers can begin to develop the critical thinking skills so important to evaluating opinionated material.

Current Controversies is also ideal for controlled research. Each anthology in the series is composed of primary sources taken from a wide gamut of informational categories including periodicals, newspapers, books, U.S. and foreign government documents, and the publications of private and public organizations. Readers will find factual support for reports, debates, and research papers covering all areas of important issues. In addition, an annotated table of contents, an index, a book and periodical bibliography, and a list of organizations to contact are included in each book to expedite further research.

Perhaps more than ever before in history, people are confronted with diverse and contradictory information. During the Persian Gulf War, for example, the public was not only treated to minute-to-minute coverage of the war, it was also inundated with critiques of the coverage and countless analyses of the factors motivating U.S. involvement. Being able to sort through the plethora of opinions accompanying today's major issues, and to draw one's own conclusions, can be a complicated and frustrating struggle. It is the editors' hope that Current Controversies will help readers with this struggle.

Introduction

"It is possible, of course, that there are
physical phenomenas that science does
not yet know about."

Until comparatively recently, health care for most people in the United States involved only standard scientifically based medical care—commonly known as conventional medicine. Since the late twentieth century, however, there has been growing interest in therapies not offered by conventional doctors; that is, therapies not derived from science, some of which are traditional in other cultures. There are many such therapies, commonly called "alternative medicine," though because in Western nations such therapies are generally used along with standard medical care, most are officially termed "complementary medicine." Collectively, they are designated complementary and alternative medicine, or CAM.

A 2007 survey showed that approximately 38 percent of American adults use some form of CAM. In 1998 the National Center for Complementary and Alternative Medicine (NCCAM) was established at the National Institutes of Health (NIH) by act of Congress. Its mission is to research complementary and alternative healing practices from a scientific perspective and to disseminate authoritative information about them to the public. However, the existence of NCCAM is controversial; many doctors, scientists, and science-oriented citizens do not believe that treatments not in accord with the known principles of biology can work. They tend to label such treatments as "quack" remedies and are opposed to any encouragement of them.

"Quack" is the wrong word to use in this context. The dictionary defines it as "a charlatan, a pretender to medical skill."

But most CAM practitioners are not pretenders; they sincerely believe that what they do helps people. There are, of course, some true quacks among them—swindlers who offer medicines or treatments they know to be worthless, just for money. However, opponents of CAM often acknowledge that many of its practitioners mean well, but nevertheless apply the word "quack" to them. For example, the American Cancer Society states, "*Quackery* refers to the promotion of methods that claim to prevent, diagnose, or cure cancers that are known to be false, or which are unproven and likely to be false. These methods are often based on theories of disease and treatment that are contrary to conventional scientific ideas." To call a treatment quackery—a word with strong negative connotation—merely because it is unproven or is based on a theory contrary to conventional science is misleading however unwise the use of unproven treatments may be.

To be sure, it is unlikely that any CAM treatment can cure cancer—claims that it can are more apt to be fraudulent than not—but that is not what CAM is generally used for. Most often, people turn to CAM not to cure serious diseases but to relieve symptoms, treat minor conditions, or achieve and maintain overall health. One reason for its growing popularity is disillusionment with the cold, impersonal attitude of modern high-tech medicine. Few patients want to be viewed as a collection of body parts in need of repair; they prefer to be seen as human beings by doctors willing to take time to talk. All forms of CAM emphasize treating the whole person—both body and mind, and often spirit—rather than just a specific illness, and their goal is to prevent more illness from occurring. Moreover, they can sometimes provide help with ongoing problems that conventional medicine has not succeeded in solving.

A small minority of CAM users do visit its practitioners for all, or nearly all, medical problems, avoiding contact with conventional medicine. This is either because they have been raised in that tradition or because they disagree with the principles on which medical science is based. They feel that the use of drugs and surgery is unnatural and does the body more harm than good. While many people view this as an ignorant belief that can and should be changed by education, it is often far deeper than that. Not everyone conforms to prevailing opinions about health, and competent adults have a constitutional right to refuse standard treatment for themselves, although not always for their children.

Do CAM healing practices work? Critics maintain that when they appear to work, it is just coincidence; supporters deny this. Certainly they are not guaranteed to work, but neither are most conventional medical treatments. The major argument against such practices is that they have not been scientifically proven. This means that the statistical likelihood of their working in any given case is unknown, but it does not necessarily mean that alternative therapies are worthless, as opponents claim they are. The mere fact that science does not understand *how* they work is not in itself evidence against them, just as personal stories of success with them are not evidence of guaranteed effectiveness.

Scientific evidence is always a matter of probability, not certainty. For example, to say that a particular medication has been proven to work does not mean that it works for everybody; it merely means that it works better than no treatment at all for a significant percentage of patients. Some older drugs, and many other standard treatments, have never been subjected to formal tests. Doctors have simply had success with them in the past.

CAM practitioners argue that their methods, too, have been successful, sometimes over a period of hundreds of years—but the reasons they give are at odds with today's science.

It is possible, of course, that there are physical phenomenas that science does not yet know about that will be discovered in the future; unexpected scientific discoveries are being made all the time. Another possibility is that the explanations given for the success of CAM healing techniques are wrong, but that their effectiveness is real. Acupuncture, for example, has traditionally been said to work by altering the flow of *chi* energy, but scientists now think it may work by releasing the body's natural painkillers, called endorphins, into the bloodstream.

Critics of CAM frequently say most if not all of its methods work no better than a placebo. Possibly this is true; but placebos—sugar pills or sham treatments—are known to work quite well. Conventional doctors used to prescribe them for minor illnesses until this was judged unethical, and they still do to some extent. For instance, doctors often give patients antibiotics for colds although colds are caused by viruses, against which antibiotics are totally ineffective. It is a surprising fact that in drug trials that involve comparing the drug to a placebo, approximately a third of the subjects responds well to the placebo. Some researchers are beginning to study the placebo effect more carefully in order to fully understand its value. The evidence shows that the human body sometimes does have the ability to self-heal—as CAM practitioners have always claimed—when a person believes that he or she is receiving treatment.

Opponents of CAM maintain that any treatment no better than a placebo is a waste of money, but this is open to question. Are the many people who request antibiotics for colds wasting their money? If the prescription helps them to recover faster than they would have without it, they are not likely to think so.

Not all forms of CAM are incompatible with science. Some, such as art and music therapy, are considered legitimate, even by those who doubt that their benefits are more than psychological. Exercise programs such as tai chi and yoga are generally viewed as helpful whether or not the philosophy underlying them is accepted. There is a wide variety of available CAM therapies, more and more of which are now being offered by conventional medical institutions. The safety and effectiveness of CAM, along with other contentious issues involving unconventional medicine, are explored and debated in *Current Controversies: Alternative Therapies.*

Is the Growing Use of Complementary and Alternative Therapies Beneficial?

Overview: What Is Complementary and Alternative Medicine?

National Center for Complementary and Alternative Medicine

The National Center for Complementary and Alternative Medicine (NCCAM), which is part of the US Department of Health and Human Services, is the federal government's lead agency for scientific research on the health care practices that are not generally considered part of conventional medicine.

Many Americans use complementary and alternative medicine (CAM) in pursuit of health and well-being. The 2007 National Health Interview Survey (NHIS), which included a comprehensive survey of CAM use by Americans, showed that approximately 38 percent of adults use CAM. This [viewpoint] presents an overview of CAM, types of CAM, summary information on safety and regulation, the mission of the National Center for Complementary and Alternative Medicine (NCCAM), and additional resources.

Defining CAM

Defining CAM is difficult, because the field is very broad and constantly changing. NCCAM defines CAM as a group of diverse medical and health care systems, practices, and products that are not generally considered part of conventional medicine. Conventional medicine (also called Western or allopathic medicine) is medicine as practiced by holders of M.D. (medical doctor) and D.O. (doctor of osteopathy) degrees and by allied health professionals, such as physical therapists, psychologists, and registered nurses. The boundaries between

"What Is Complementary and Alternative Medicine?" National Center for Complementary and Alternative Medicine, April 2010.

CAM and conventional medicine are not absolute, and specific CAM practices may, over time, become widely accepted.

"Complementary medicine" refers to use of CAM *together with* conventional medicine, such as using acupuncture in addition to usual care to help lessen pain. Most use of CAM by Americans is complementary. "Alternative medicine" refers to use of CAM *in place of* conventional medicine. "Integrative medicine" (also called integrated medicine) refers to a practice that combines both conventional and CAM treatments for which there is evidence of safety and effectiveness.

Types of CAM

CAM practices are often grouped into broad categories, such as natural products, mind-body medicine, and manipulative and body-based practices. Although these categories are not formally defined, they are useful for discussing CAM practices. Some CAM practices may fit into more than one category.

Natural Products

This area of CAM includes use of a variety of herbal medicines (also known as botanicals), vitamins, minerals, and other "natural products." Many are sold over the counter as *dietary supplements*. (Some uses of dietary supplements—e.g., taking a multivitamin to meet minimum daily nutritional requirements or taking calcium to promote bone health—are not thought of as CAM.)

CAM "natural products" also include *probiotics*—live microorganisms (usually bacteria) that are similar to microorganisms normally found in the human digestive tract and that may have beneficial effects. Probiotics are available in foods (e.g., yogurts) or as dietary supplements. They are not the same thing as prebiotics—non-digestible food ingredients that selectively stimulate the growth and/or activity of microorganisms already present in the body.

Historical note: Herbal or botanical medicines reflect some of the first attempts to improve the human condition. The personal effects of the mummified prehistoric "ice man" found in the Italian Alps in 1991 included medicinal herbs. By the Middle Ages, thousands of botanical products had been inventoried for their medicinal effects.

Current use: Interest in and use of CAM natural products have grown considerably in the past few decades. The 2007 NHIS found that 17.7 percent of American adults had used a non-vitamin/non-mineral natural product. These products were the most popular form of CAM among both adults and children. The most commonly used product among adults was fish oil/omega 3s (reported by 37.4 percent of all adults who said they used natural products); popular products for children included echinacea (37.2 percent) and fish oil/omega 3s (30.5 percent).

Whole medical systems, which are complete systems of theory and practice that have evolved over time in different cultures and apart from conventional or Western medicine, may be considered CAM.

Mind-Body Medicine

Mind-body practices focus on the interactions among the brain, mind, body, and behavior, with the intent to use the mind to affect physical functioning and promote health. Many CAM practices embody this concept—in different ways.

- *Meditation* techniques include specific postures, focused attention, or an open attitude toward distractions. People use meditation to increase calmness and relaxation, improve psychological balance, cope with illness, or enhance overall health and well-being.

- The various styles of *yoga* used for health purposes typically combine physical postures, breathing techniques, and meditation or relaxation. People use yoga as part of a general health regimen, and also for a variety of health conditions.

- *Acupuncture* is a family of procedures involving the stimulation of specific points on the body using a variety of techniques, such as penetrating the skin with needles that are then manipulated by hand or by electrical stimulation. It is one of the key components of traditional Chinese medicine, and is among the oldest healing practices in the world. (Acupuncture is considered to be a part of mind-body medicine, but it is also a component of energy medicine, manipulative and body-based practices, and traditional Chinese medicine.)

Other examples of mind-body practices include *deep-breathing exercises, guided imagery, hypnotherapy, progressive relaxation, qigong,* and *tai chi.*

Historical note: The concept that the mind is important in the treatment of illness is integral to the healing approaches of traditional Chinese medicine and Ayurvedic medicine [traditional system of medicine in India], dating back more than 2,000 years. Hippocrates [considered the father of Western medicine] also noted the moral and spiritual aspects of healing and believed that treatment could occur only with consideration of attitude, environmental influences, and natural remedies.

Current use: Several mind-body approaches ranked among the top 10 CAM practices reported by adults in the 2007 NHIS. For example, the survey found that 12.7 percent of adults had used deep-breathing exercises, 9.4 percent had practiced meditation, and 6.1 percent had practiced yoga; use of these three CAM practices had increased significantly since the previous (2002) NHIS. Progressive relaxation and guided imagery were also among the top 10 CAM therapies for adults;

deep breathing and yoga ranked high among children. Acupuncture had been used by 1.4 percent of adults and 0.2 percent of children.

Manipulative and Body-Based Practices

Manipulative and body-based practices focus primarily on the structures and systems of the body, including the bones and joints, soft tissues, and circulatory and lymphatic systems. Two commonly used therapies fall within this category:

- *Spinal manipulation* is performed by chiropractors and by other health care professionals such as physical therapists, osteopaths, and some conventional medical doctors. Practitioners use their hands or a device to apply a controlled force to a joint of the spine, moving it beyond its passive range of motion; the amount of force applied depends on the form of manipulation used. Spinal manipulation is among the treatment options used by people with low-back pain—a very common condition that can be difficult to treat.

- The term *massage therapy* encompasses many different techniques. In general, therapists press, rub, and otherwise manipulate the muscles and other soft tissues of the body. People use massage for a variety of health-related purposes, including to relieve pain, rehabilitate sports injuries, reduce stress, increase relaxation, address anxiety and depression, and aid general well-being.

Historical note: Spinal manipulation has been used since the time of the ancient Greeks and was incorporated into chiropractic and osteopathic medicine in the late 19th century. Massage therapy dates back thousands of years. References to massage appear in writings from ancient China, Japan, India, Arabic nations, Egypt, Greece (Hippocrates defined medicine as "the art of rubbing"), and Rome.

Current use: According to the 2007 NHIS, chiropractic/osteopathic manipulation and massage ranked in the top 10 CAM therapies among both adults and children. The survey found that 8.6 percent of adults and 2.8 percent of children had used chiropractic or osteopathic manipulation, and 8.3 percent of adults and 1 percent of children had used massage.

Other CAM Practices

CAM also encompasses *movement therapies*—a broad range of Eastern and Western movement-based approaches used to promote physical, mental, emotional, and spiritual well-being. Examples include *Feldenkrais method, Alexander technique, Pilates,* and *Trager psychophysical integration.* According to the 2007 NHIS, 1.5 percent of adults and 0.4 percent of children used movement therapies.

Rigorous, well-designed clinical trials for many CAM therapies are often lacking; therefore, the safety and effectiveness of many CAM therapies are uncertain.

Practices of *traditional healers* can also be considered a form of CAM. Traditional healers use methods based on indigenous theories, beliefs, and experiences handed down from generation to generation. A familiar example in the United States is the Native American healer/medicine man. The 2007 NHIS found that 0.4 percent of adults and 1.1 percent of children had used a traditional healer (usage varied for the seven specific types of healers identified in the survey).

Some CAM practices involve manipulation of various *energy* fields to affect health. Such fields may be characterized as veritable (measurable) or putative (yet to be measured). Practices based on veritable forms of energy include those involving electromagnetic fields (e.g., *magnet therapy* and *light therapy*). Practices based on putative energy fields (also called biofields) generally reflect the concept that human beings are infused with subtle forms of energy; *qigong*, *Reiki*, and *healing touch* are examples of such practices. The 2007 NHIS found relatively low use of putative energy therapies. Only 0.5 percent of adults and 0.2 percent of children had used energy healing/Reiki (the survey defined energy healing as the channeling of healing energy through the hands of a practitioner into the client's body).

Finally, *whole medical systems*, which are complete systems of theory and practice that have evolved over time in different cultures and apart from conventional or Western medicine, may be considered CAM. Examples of ancient whole medical systems include *Ayurvedic medicine* and *traditional Chinese medicine*. More modern systems that have developed in the past few centuries include *homeopathy* and *naturopathy*. The 2007 NHIS asked about the use of Ayurveda, homeopathy, and naturopathy. Although relatively few respondents said they had used Ayurveda or naturopathy, homeopathy ranked 10th in usage among adults (1.8 percent) and 5th among children (1.3 percent).

A Note About Safety and Effectiveness

Rigorous, well-designed clinical trials for many CAM therapies are often lacking; therefore, the safety and effectiveness of many CAM therapies are uncertain. NCCAM is sponsoring research designed to fill this knowledge gap by building a scientific evidence base about CAM therapies—whether they are safe; and whether they work for the conditions for which people use them and, if so, how they work.

As with any medical treatment, there can be risks with CAM therapies. These general precautions can help to minimize risks:

- Select CAM practitioners with care. Find out about the practitioner's training and experience.

- Be aware that some dietary supplements may interact with medications or other supplements, may have side effects of their own, or may contain potentially harmful ingredients not listed on the label. Also keep in mind that most supplements have not been tested in pregnant women, nursing mothers, or children.

• Tell all your health care providers about any complementary and alternative practices you use. Give them a full picture of what you do to manage your health. This will help ensure coordinated and safe care.

Cost-Effective Alternative Therapies Are Being Employed by Integrative Medicine

Deepak Chopra, Dean Ornish, Rustum Roy, and Andrew Weil

Deepak Chopra, Dean Ornish, and Andrew Weil are all prominent physicians in the field of integrative medicine and individually have written many popular books about it. Rustum Roy was a science policy analyst and advocate of alternative medicine.

In mid-February [2009] the Institute of Medicine of the National Academy of Sciences and the Bravewell Collaborative are convening a "Summit on Integrative Medicine and the Health of the Public." This is a watershed in the evolution of integrative medicine, a holistic approach to health care that uses the best of conventional and alternative therapies such as meditation, yoga, acupuncture and herbal remedies. Many of these therapies are now scientifically documented to be not only medically effective but also cost effective.

President-elect Barack Obama and former Sen. Tom Daschle (the nominee for Secretary of Health and Human Services) understand that if we want to make affordable health care available to the 45 million Americans who do not have health insurance, then we need to address the fundamental causes of health and illness, and provide incentives for healthy ways of living rather than reimbursing only drugs and surgery.

Heart disease, diabetes, prostate cancer, breast cancer and obesity account for 75% of health-care costs, and yet these are largely preventable and even reversible by changing diet and lifestyle. As Mr. Obama states in his health plan, unveiled dur-

Deepak Chopra, Dean Ornish, Rustum Roy, and Andrew Weil, "'Alternative' Medicine Is Mainstream," *Wall Street Journal*, January 9, 2009. Reprinted with permission from The Wall Street Journal, © 2009 Dow Jones & Company. All rights reserved.

ing his campaign: "This nation is facing a true epidemic of chronic disease. An increasing number of Americans are suffering and dying needlessly from diseases such as obesity, diabetes, heart disease, asthma and HIV/AIDS, all of which can be delayed in onset if not prevented entirely."

Capacity to Heal

The latest scientific studies show that our bodies have a remarkable capacity to begin healing, and much more quickly than we had once realized, if we address the lifestyle factors that often cause these chronic diseases. These studies show that integrative medicine can make a powerful difference in our health and well-being, how quickly these changes may occur, and how dynamic these mechanisms can be.

Many people tend to think of breakthroughs in medicine as a new drug, laser or high-tech surgical procedure. They often have a hard time believing that the simple choices that we make in our lifestyle—what we eat, how we respond to stress, whether or not we smoke cigarettes, how much exercise we get, and the quality of our relationships and social support— can be as powerful as drugs and surgery. But they often are. And in many instances, they're even more powerful.

A recent study published in the Proceedings of the National Academy of Sciences *found that [lifestyle] approaches may even change gene expression in hundreds of genes in only a few months.*

These studies often used high-tech, state-of-the-art measures to prove the power of simple, low-tech, and low-cost interventions. Integrative medicine approaches such as plant-based diets, yoga, meditation and psychosocial support may stop or even reverse the progression of coronary heart disease, diabetes, hypertension, prostate cancer, obesity, hypercholesterolemia and other chronic conditions.

31

A recent study published in the *Proceedings of the National Academy of Sciences* found that these approaches may even change gene expression in hundreds of genes in only a few months. Genes associated with cancer, heart disease and inflammation were downregulated or "turned off" whereas protective genes were upregulated or "turned on." A study published in the *Lancet Oncology* reported that these changes increase telomerase, the enzyme that lengthens telomeres, the ends of our chromosomes that control how long we live. Even drugs have not been shown to do this.

Unwarranted Costs

Our "health-care system" is primarily a disease-care system. Last year, $2.1 trillion was spent in the U.S. on medical care, or 16.5% of the gross national product. Of these trillions, 95 cents of every dollar was spent to treat disease *after* it had already occurred. At least 75% of these costs were spent on treating chronic diseases, such as heart disease and diabetes, that are preventable or even reversible.

The choices are especially clear in cardiology. In 2006, for example, according to data provided by the American Heart Association, 1.3 million coronary angioplasty procedures were performed at an average cost of $48,399 each, or more than $60 billion; and 448,000 coronary bypass operations were performed at a cost of $99,743 each, or more than $44 billion. In other words, Americans spent more than $100 billion in 2006 for these two procedures alone.

Despite these costs, a randomized controlled trial published in April 2007 in the *New England Journal of Medicine* found that angioplasties and stents do not prolong life or even prevent heart attacks in stable patients (i.e., 95% of those who receive them). Coronary bypass surgery prolongs life in less than 3% of patients who receive it. So, Medicare and other insurers and individuals pay billions for surgical procedures like angioplasty and bypass surgery that are usually dangerous, invasive, expensive and largely ineffective. Yet they pay very little—if any money at all—for integrative medicine approaches that have been proven to reverse and prevent most chronic diseases that account for at least 75% of health-care costs. The INTERHEART study, published in September 2004 in the *Lancet*, followed 30,000 men and women on six continents and found that changing lifestyle could prevent at least 90% of all heart disease.

That bears repeating: The disease that accounts for more premature deaths and costs Americans more than any other illness is almost completely preventable simply by changing diet and lifestyle. And the same lifestyle changes that can prevent or even reverse heart disease also help prevent or reverse many other chronic diseases as well. Chronic pain is one of the major sources of workers' compensation claims costs, yet studies show that it is often susceptible to acupuncture and Qigong [alternative therapy that includes meditation, controlled breathing, and movement exercises]. Herbs usually have far fewer side effects than pharmaceuticals.

It's time to move past the debate of alternative medicine versus traditional medicine, and to focus on what works, what doesn't, for whom, and under which circumstances.

Living Better

Joy, pleasure and freedom are sustainable, deprivation and austerity are not. When you eat a healthier diet, quit smoking, exercise, meditate and have more love in your life, then your brain receives more blood and oxygen, so you think more clearly, have more energy, need less sleep. Your brain may grow so many new neurons that it could get measurably bigger in only a few months. Your face gets more blood flow, so your skin glows more and wrinkles less. Your heart gets more blood flow, so you have more stamina and can even begin to reverse heart disease. Your sexual organs receive more blood flow, so you may become more potent—similar to the way that circulation-increasing drugs like Viagra work. For many people, these are choices worth making—not just to live longer, but also to live better.

It's time to move past the debate of alternative medicine versus traditional medicine, and to focus on what works, what doesn't, for whom, and under which circumstances. It will take serious government funding to find out, but these findings may help reduce costs and increase health.

Integrative medicine approaches bring together those in red states and blue states, liberals and conservatives, Democrats and Republicans, because these are human issues. They are both medically effective and, important in our current economic climate, cost effective. These approaches emphasize both personal responsibility and the opportunity to make affordable, quality health care available to those who most need it. Mr. Obama should make them an integral part of his health plan as soon as possible.

Alternative Therapies Do Good but Should Not Be Integrated with Conventional Medicine

Bruce G. Charlton

Bruce G. Charlton is a professor of theoretical medicine at the University of Buckingham in England.

I wish to suggest a new way of considering alternative and complementary therapies. Common attitudes towards alternative therapies tend to be polarized into two extreme views. The first view is that alternative therapies do good for many people and so they should therefore be integrated with orthodox medicine. The second, and opposite view, is that alternative therapies are worthless or harmful and they should be ignored or eradicated. A third position is that alternative therapies may or may not do good, and this should be decided using the methods of medical science.

I believe that all three of these views are mistaken. My interpretation is 1. Alternative therapies indeed do good for many people. 2. From a strictly medical perspective they are worthless. 3. Alternative therapies should not be integrated with orthodox medicine. 4. They cannot meaningfully be investigated using the methods of medical science. Because alternative therapies do not 'cure' disease, they have no role in orthodox medicine; and because they are explained non-scientifically, they cannot be evaluated using the criteria of medical science.

My suggestion is that alternative therapies should be regarded as spiritual practices, linked to the phenomenon of New Age spirituality. This is a valid benefit in the modern world. But the benefit is psychological not medical. Alternative therapies are about making people feel better ('healing') not about mending their dysfunctional brains and bodies ('curing').

Alternative therapies are about making people feel better ('healing') not about mending their dysfunctional brains and bodies ('curing').

Differences Between Alternative Therapies and Orthodox Medicine

I would define alternative therapies in terms of them having non-scientific explanations. In so far as a therapy does have a biological explanation, I would regard that therapy as simply part of orthodox medicine. The crucial difference between orthodox and alternative therapies is therefore that alternative medical systems have non-scientific explanations based on spiritual, mystical, legendary or otherwise intuitively appealing insights.

This difference between orthodox and alternative medicine can be illustrated with an example. In orthodox medicine, the illness of 'hypertension' or high blood pressure is explained in terms of a mass of interlinked biological knowledge concerning the structure and function of the human body including heart and arteries and the functional relationship between blood pressure and diseases such as stroke. Treatment of hypertension is based on a detailed scientific understanding of how the heart and arteries are regulated by the nervous system, and how this can be modified using drugs. The fact that orthodox therapies are embedded in standard biological science is what makes them scientifically testable.

By contrast, acupuncture is based around the existence of meridians, which are structures described in historic medical and religious literature but not detectable using scientific equipment. If the theory of acupuncture does not actually contradict modern biological science, then it has nothing to do with it.

In homeopathy the mechanism of action is based on a 'magical' form of reasoning—the 'law of similars', or like-cures-like—which has no basis in modern therapeutics. Another homeopathic principle, that of increasing potency of a medicine with increasing dilution (so long as dilution is done in a particular way called succussion) is in contradiction with modern chemistry. So the theories of homeopathy flatly contradict modern pharmacology.

And in chiropractic medicine, the presumed spinal vertebral subluxations which are supposed to cause disease are not visible using imaging technologies such as X-rays or MRI scans. The key diagnostic features of chiropractic medicine are therefore based on a theory derived from intuition, rather than science.

There is not one clear-cut instance in which any alternative therapy is unequivocally effective and indicated for any particular disease or symptom.

Yet acupuncture, homeopathy and chiropractic are among the most professionalized of alternative therapies—the explanatory theories for crystal healing or aromatherapy are even more imaginative and less scientific. The conclusion is that alternative medical systems are disconnected from the knowledge and practices of modern science.

Alternative therapies are similarly disconnected from orthodox medicine. Despite many decades or centuries of experience, there is not one clear-cut instance in which any alternative therapy is unequivocally effective and indicated for any particular disease or symptom. There are no cures of the otherwise incurable—nobody dragged back from certain death in the way that has happened many millions of times with antibiotics and steroids. Severed limbs are not reattached to bodies, nor diseased internal organs extracted, nor (despite the misleading political propaganda for acupuncture) can reliable anaesthesia be induced.

It is noticeable that the only positive trials in alternative therapies have been reported for conditions characterized by very unpredictable and reversible symptoms such as those that occur in hay fever, rhinitis, asthma, eczema, back pain, arthritic pain, migraine, chronic fatigue, post-operative ileus, and multiple sclerosis. These are conditions where it is hard to prove that anything works, where factors such as the placebo effect play a large role and where subtle biases or errors in experimental design (and publication) can most easily generate falsely positive results.

In order to design experiments to test a therapy, the therapy needs a scientific explanation; and when this is lacking there are problems—even in orthodox medicine. When orthodox medical treatments have proven effectiveness in the usual randomized clinical trials but lack an accepted scientific explanation, then the results of these trials tend to be regarded with suspicion. . . .

What Is New Age Spirituality?

I have said that alternative therapies are not a part of science, but should instead be considered part of New Age spirituality—however, the meaning of 'New Age' may require further explanation.

New Age spirituality is a very broadly defined term which tends to be used to refer to people who overtly adopt an 'alternative' or 'green' lifestyle, which evolved from the hippies of the late 1960s. And surveys have shown that alternative therapies are indeed very popular among this group. But the typical New Age style of spirituality is, in fact, much more widespread than this minority counter-culture fringe, indeed New Age practices involve perhaps the majority of the population in modernizing societies.

The New Age focuses on subjective psychological states such as integration, authenticity and self-expression. If traditional religion can be seen as a combination of spirituality and church (i.e., a formal institutional structure) then New Age can be conceptualized as individual spirituality separate from churches. In the past, spirituality was controlled by churches, and the forms and practices of spirituality were restricted. New Age really is something new, a product of modern individuals, and the lifestyle was not possible in earlier and less complex stages of society.

Essentially, New Age consists of individuals pursuing their own spiritual goals in their own way. They make evaluations based upon what kinds of spiritual benefit they want, and what is effective in achieving these benefits. . . .

Almost any object or stimulus might count as New Age healing: What matters is the subjective 'meaning' to the individual—the self-evaluated effect it has on a person's sense of well-being.

Orthodox medicine must cure, and should aim to heal— but does not need to heal; while alternative therapies do not cure—so they must heal in order to be worthwhile.

The Value of Healing Versus Curing

Alternative therapies are often advertised as 'healing', and this word can be interpreted as referring to personal, subjective and psychological benefits. Any specific alternative therapy may or may not benefit any particular individual in this psychological sense. But the range of alternative therapies is very large, and continually growing. Among this vast choice of therapies it is likely that an individual can find some which harmonize with his or her own spiritual goals.

By contrast, orthodox medicine is focused upon curing disease—in which the disease and the cure tend to be defined as objectively and scientifically as possible. The treatment of diabetes focuses on controlling the measured levels of blood sugar, the treatment of pneumonia is focused upon killing the causal germs as detected by laboratory studies. It is naturally desirable that a diabetic or pneumonia patient also be 'healed' in the sense of made to feel subjectively better—but even when this does not happen, the scientific 'cure' is worth having. So, orthodox medicine must cure, and should aim to heal—but does not need to heal; while alternative therapies do not cure—so they must heal in order to be worthwhile.

Because they aim to heal, the explanations of alternative medicine need to have intuitive appeal: They are mythic explanations, not accounts of scientific causality. Myths are stories which function as poetic symbols, and not as literal signs. Myths are meant to imply many things (not just one thing), and have a personal meaning (rather than be an objective description). Scientific theories are not myths—they are intended to be precise descriptions with narrowly defined meanings.

For example, the meridians of acupuncture have no literal scientific signification. But meridians are suggestive poetic symbols of the way that life can be experienced as a flow of energies, the fact that these energies may come into conflict (yin and yang) and the need for these energies to be balanced. The oriental basis of acupuncture may also appeal, and the precision (and frisson of fear, which must be overcome) of the needle insertion technique may also be intuitively pleasing. If so, then acupuncture might be chosen as one part of a lifestyle.

As another example, perhaps the commonest theme in alternative therapies concerns 'energy'. But this is 'energy' as a positive subjective sense of vitality and harmony—it has nothing to do with the concept of energy as measured by scientific technologies. Indeed, in alternative medicine, the term 'energy' has a multifaceted, metaphorical quality which stands in stark contrast to the equations of physics.

But another individual may dislike or fail to be engaged by oriental themes, or may find needles too scary, and may instead find a spiritual benefit from contemplating stone age rock carvings or cave paintings. This person might find that healing rituals involving beautiful crystals produce the psychological effects they seek. Healing crystals come with poetic descriptions of the expected effect of each type of crystal, and ways in which they might be deployed to generate these effects.

A person either finds an intuitive plausibility to these descriptions of crystal healing, or they do not. Someone who likes the idea of crystals can try out the rituals, and if this has the desired effect they might continue to do them; but if the rituals don't make the person feel any better, or make them feel worse, then they will presumably give up crystal healing and might try something else instead—such as aromatherapy, colours, runes, flowers or herbs.

> *Because New Age healing is based upon individual feelings it is inappropriate (indeed potentially dangerous) when applied to such matters of public policy as science . . . or medicine.*

The Impossibility of Integration

Because New Age healing is based upon individual feelings it is inappropriate (indeed potentially dangerous) when applied to such matters of public policy as science, technology, law, economics—or medicine. But so long as New Age reasoning stays away from these objective areas, its subjective evaluations may have great personal value.

Also, this subjective evaluation system makes New Age healing immune to challenge by science or medicine. New Age validity is a matter of what 'works for me'; contradiction from other people is redefined as 'your truth'. Individual experience is the ultimate authority, and if an individual claims that they find an alternative therapy to be effective in achieving subjective spiritual goals such as personal harmony and growth, then there can be no argument from medicine or biology. If someone feels energized by an alternative therapy and gains a more positive attitude towards life, then this subjective perception is just as valid as artistic appreciation, preferences among foods or selection of fashions. And the wide range of choice, competition and continual innovation in New Age systems of healing ensures that there is little chance of the public becoming habituated or fatigued by the stimuli on offer—there is always something novel to experience.

New Age spiritualities—including alternative systems of healing—constitute a vast resource of ideas and stimuli, and fulfill a range of useful functions. New Age ideas are published and disseminated widely, for instance in the 'mind, body and spirit' sections of bookshops, in the broadcast mass media and on the Internet. People are free to 'opt-in' to the extent that they find ideas helpful, and are free to ignore anything they do not.

The simultaneous growth of modern medicine and the New Age implies that consumers of alternative healing nearly always use these therapies broadly appropriately: i.e., for the attainment of subjective personal and spiritual goals, and not for the treatment of diseases. The relationship between orthodox and alternative therapies is therefore potentially a harmonious one.

But clashes are inevitable when both sides claim interpretative authority over the same situation. The major source of conflict is when alternative healing practitioners make claims which purport to be factual but are scientifically incredible.

The dilemma is that in the short term a modicum of science (or pseudoscience) may serve to increase the status of New Age practitioners and validate their activities. Yet, in the longer term, the attempt to subordinate science to spirituality will lead to a conflict which science will win.

Scientists and orthodox physicians who are rightly dismissive of bogus claims to objective effectiveness may in turn deny the subjective benefits of alternative therapies. The situation occurs when medical scientists misunderstand claims of 'healing' as claims of curing disease; or when they try to literalize and ridicule mythic explanations such as the imaginative descriptions of crystal therapy. But this is as misconceived as evaluating the factual accuracy of a poetic metaphor. When Shakespeare asked his mistress: 'Shall I compare thee to a summer's day?', he was not making an equation between the beloved and warm climactic conditions. Contemporary alternative healing is an unstable mixture of science and spirituality. In the future it would be better if these incompatible elements would separate out.

Randomized trials of New Age therapies are as inappropriate as randomized trials of prayer or the enjoyment of Mozart.

The Benefits of Separation

Alternative medicine will survive and grow most effectively by dropping its scientific pretensions; and becoming candidly mythic, poetic, fictive, symbolic, metaphorical and fantasy based. This process is already well advanced in other aspects of New Age spirituality where an explicit appeal to subjective intuition is made.

Orthodox medicine and alternative healing cannot and should not become integrated, for precisely the reason that they are totally different forms of activity with different rules and purposes. To integrate would be to damage what is valuable in each. Randomized trials of New Age therapies are as inappropriate as randomized trials of prayer or the enjoyment of Mozart—such investigations will inevitably be inconclusive, confusing and irrelevant. . . .

New Age healing deploys the placebo effect and the personality of the therapist in a much freer and more powerful way than can be achieved in orthodox medicine. Alternative healers will be impaired if required to work within strict theoretical and organizational confines. When healing depends on therapeutic charisma, professional and standardized forms of education and accreditation will just tend to weed out some of the most potentially helpful personalities. . . .

In situations where clients consult with alternative therapists, it is likely that the role of charisma has a vital part to play. A popular therapist will probably have a 'therapeutic personality' such that personal interaction makes most clients feel better. But personality clashes are inevitable, even for a highly charismatic healer, which is why wide choice and client control of the consultation is of such great importance in alternative therapy.

It is a great advantage if orthodox medicine is practiced by charismatic doctors. But with orthodox medicine, charisma is an optional extra: The medicine will still work in its absence.

In orthodox medicine things are different. A physician may try to present the standard scientific explanation underlying therapy in an intuitively appealing way—but even if this attempt fails, the treatment should still be useful since its effectiveness has typically been objectively evaluated. Surgery or chemotherapy may make the patient feel much worse in the short term, even when they succeed in curing cancer. Of course, it is a great advantage if orthodox medicine is practiced by charismatic doctors. But with orthodox medicine, charisma is an optional extra: The medicine will still work in its absence.

But there are no objective boundaries on the explanations offered by alternative therapists, or provided with New Age products, because clients vary so widely in what they find convincing. In alternative healing, the explanation must be intuitively appealing to the client, here and now, or else the therapy will not succeed in making the client feel better. Indeed, so long as the therapy does no significant harm, intuitive benefit is the beginning and end of evaluation in alternative medicine.

I envisage a future in which orthodox and alternative therapies both thrive, but separately. Orthodox medicine is based on scientific theories and is characterized by objective evaluation criteria and formal professional structures of education and certification. In contrast, alternative healing deploys a wide range of intuitively appealing but non-scientific explanations, and constitutes a consumer-dominated marketplace of ideas and therapies which are personally evaluated by the client.

Orthodox medicine focuses on curing disease and promoting health. But alternative therapies should instead be focused on promoting well-being and personal fulfillment. To accomplish this, alternative therapists need to be able freely to deploy personal charisma and richly mythic explanations. In conclusion, alternative therapies are neither medical nor scientific, but they should be respected as a potential contribution to modern spiritual well-being.

Complementary and Alternative Therapies Are Helpful Even if They Are Placebos

William Grassie

William Grassie is the founding executive director of the Metanexus Institute, which studies the relationship between religion and science from a global perspective. He is the author of several books.

I have a cold this week and my back hurts again. I hate being sick and I don't suffer well, but sooner or later this is what life holds in store for each of us. It's said there's no avoiding death and taxes, and both are sure to go up with the spiraling cost of health care and the aging of the boomers.

More and more people are dissatisfied with health care in the United States. According to a 2009 NIH [National Institutes of Health] study, Americans spent $34 billion on complementary and alternative medicine (CAM), accounting for 11.2 percent of total out-of-pocket expenditures on health care. Is this wasted money? Does prayer heal? Does homeopathy work? Is acupuncture effective? Is Ayurvedic medicine [traditional medicine of India that is considered an alternative therapy by Western medicine] really medicine at all? And what should I do about my lower-back pain and stuffed-up nose?

Most physicians trained in modern scientific medicine are quite skeptical of CAM and other spirituality-based healing practices, but contemporary research points increasingly to what we might call the deep semiotics of health. It seems, minimally, that hope helps to heal. And ritualized hope in groups heals more effectively.

Recognizing the Signs and Symbols of Health

Semiotics, of course, is the study of signs and symbols, but it really has nothing to do with the fictional "symbologist" character played by Tom Hanks in Dan Brown's *The Da Vinci Code*. Semiotics is mostly dense philosophy and linguistics with a dash of neuroscience thrown in.

Psychosomatic effects are involved in all medical therapies, whether they are orthodox scientific or alternative healing practices.

The deep semiotics of health is an attempt to recognize the signs and symbols of health and to take control over the largely unconscious processes that affect our minds-brains-bodies. The mash up of these terms is necessary in light of contemporary science. Let me explain.

Psychosomatic effects are involved in all medical therapies, whether they are orthodox scientific or alternative healing practices. There are now several decades of placebo studies to validate this fact, including measurable biochemical responses in subjects; most notably in releasing endogenous opiates in the brain for pain relief.

To these we can add new insights about how our mental states can influence our immune systems and regulate powerful hormones in our bodies. Too much mental stress, for instance, releases cortisol in our bloodstream—a powerful steroid that, over time, weakens our immune system.

Psychosomatic effects are not really isolated in individual patients, as physicians tend to assume: a better term instead might be psychosocial somatic effects. Try saying "psychosocial somatic effects" ten times fast with a runny nose—keep the tissues handy.

Epidemiological studies and mathematical models of "social contagion" further reveal that positive and negative behaviors and attitudes, including many indicators of physical health, can travel indirectly through communities and social networks, though we don't actually understand how this happens.

These effects only work because of complex social and cultural interactions over the course of a lifetime. Popping pills, white coats, stethoscopes, and the examination room are all symbols in the liturgy of sickness and healing. They're reinforced from childhood with the rituals of visits to doctors and pharmacists, the act of taking pills at home, and television medical dramas from *Doctor Kildare* to *ER*. In Chinese culture, acupuncture is similarly reinforced and encoded as effective therapy. Antibiotics, and apparently also acupuncture, work regardless of your belief system—but they work better if you believe in them.

There is nothing wrong with a good placebo, especially when you choose it yourself.

Double-Blind Trials

The history of medicine up until the last century was essentially the history of the placebo effect. Double-blind, randomized control trials are now the gold standard in medical research and have only been widely used for the last fifty-odd years. It is a research protocol that works especially well for pharmaceutical products where taking a pill or an injection is the intervention, but designing such studies for acupuncture, chiropractics, or even back surgery is no easy matter. Double-blind experiments have blinded researchers to the profoundly psychosocial somatic dimensions of human health.

Calling something a placebo, in turn, is widely perceived to be a criticism or even an insult in the contemporary research climate; but there is nothing wrong with a good placebo, especially when you choose it yourself. The cup of herbal tea I'm drinking may have no pharmacological effect: I might just as well drink hot water. But the herbal aroma sure makes me think and feel like I am getting better.

Placebos may be the most effective and important tool in any healer's toolbox, though they certainly raise complex medical and ethical problems. Informed consent, for instance, should still guide medical ethics. Substituting sham treatments for an effective, known treatment for a serious illness is always out of bounds. The good news, however, is that patients can and should be informed about the benefits of a holistic approach that includes CAM and other spiritually based interventions of their own choosing. These should be seen as a supplement to known effective treatments developed by scientific medicine. I still plan to take NyQuil tonight. But, now, CAM healing deserves to be taken seriously as part of the mix.

Spiritual healers and CAM practitioners don't think of themselves as mere placebo providers. These practices have been developed over thousands of years of human experimentation in diverse cultures. There may be scientific reasons why some of these CAM therapies work, just as some of what is practiced under the rubric of Western, physicalist medicine is not really evidence based, but an ongoing experiment with only probabilistic results and unknown long-term consequences.

The impact of much of CAM . . . is partially, probably, and perhaps predominantly psychosocial somatic—but so are all medical therapies.

There may be some important discoveries for science to sift out from the enormous diversity of traditional medications and procedures. Hot baths, extra sleep, and chicken soup all turn out to have explainable benefits for my current condition, for instance. The impact of much of CAM, however, is partially, probably, and perhaps predominantly psychosocial somatic—but so are all medical therapies, to varying degree, including my blue-green, foul-tasting NyQuil. In cases where physicalist medicine offers no cure for chronic and life-threatening illnesses, CAM therapies and their spiritual cousins do provide at least a kind of relief for suffering patients, and maybe much more.

The More Elaborate the Ritual, the More Effective the Placebo

Is there a way to systematically individualize, ritualize, and harness psychosocial somatic interventions as a supplement to standard treatments? This would require clinicians to customize the context of health care to the culture and beliefs of each particular patient. They could also try to utilize larger social networks as part of the intervention for the patient; both inside the medical institution and outside, among the patient's friends and family. The wisdom of CAM and spiritual interventions is that the more elaborate the healing ritual, the more effective the placebo effect. Supplementing physicalist medicine in this holistic way might improve health outcomes by thirty percent or more if placebo studies can be generalized and averaged out across disease types.

The best medical science is now supplemented by the wisdom of the ages—wisdom which also turns out now to have at least some scientific basis. The ancient physician Galen noted, "He cures most successfully in whom the people have the most confidence." Even the modern CAM debunker [R.] Barker Bausell curiously ends his book, *Snake Oil Science*, by advising his readers on how to select a placebo therapy that works. "Once you've started the therapy," he writes, "embrace it . . . with all your heart and soul." After three days of blowing my nose and feeling lousy, I might just try some of that snake oil.

Complementary and Alternative Therapies Are Based on Pseudoscience

Narendra Nayak

Narendra Nayak is a retired professor of biochemistry from Mangalore, India. He is the president of the Federation of Indian Rationalist Associations and has been featured on many television programs.

When most people hear the term *'Alternative Medicine'* they tend to think that it is used to describe something that offers a tested, tried alternative to mainstream systems of medicine. In India we have three types of systems of treatment and diagnosis—the recognized evidence-based one—the scientific system; the recognized but not evidence-based ones under the acronym AYUSH—Ayurveda, Unani, Siddha and Homeopathy; and the third has a list that is almost never complete but contains common ones like electrohomeopathy, reiki, pranic healing, aromatherapy, music therapy, gem therapy, etc. The term 'alternative medicine' perhaps describes best the last class. (Note: Technically all those systems of treatment and diagnosis that are not science-based are designated as 'Alternative Medicine', but in the Indian context there are three categories because of the government's endorsement of AYUSH.) The third class labeled 'Alternative Medicine' in India seems to be the favourite hunting ground for quacks of all types.

Development of Modern Medicine

The scientific system of medicine is popularly known as *'allopathy'* in India, a term that was coined a long time ago by the inventor of *homeopathy*, a German called [Samuel] Hahne-

Narendra Nayak, "Why 'Alternative Medicine' Is Neither Science-Based Nor Medicine," *Nirmukta*, August 30, 2010. www.nirmukta.com. Reproduced by permission.

mann. Outside of India the term 'allopathy' is rarely used to-day. [It is increasingly used in the United States by advocates of alternatives.] In the early 20th century Hahnemann pro-posed that minute doses of the very same substances that cause the symptoms of a particular disease in a healthy indi-vidual could cure that disease. This he called homeopathy. Since the other system of medicine prevalent at that time claimed otherwise, it was called allopathy or the other. At that time this system of medicine involved treatments like purging, bleeding, leech therapy, injections with toxic substances, etc. The side effects of these were so unpleasant that the patient many a time would be better off without the treatment! By contrast homeopathy involved treatment with sugar pills and tinctures whose active ingredients, if any, were milk, sugar and ethanol respectively. None of these could be harmful to nor-mal people unless they were lactose intolerant! That explains why homeopathy became very popular! Those were times when no treatment at all was often better than drastic treat-ment and the mortality rate was higher after treatment with the remedies described above under allopathy! Nomenclature apart, it was this system that developed into modern medi-cine, as it was not based on any irrefutable dogma and is sub-ject to self-correction (the scientific method). Things that were the norm at one time got discarded when more sophisti-cated investigative methods showed that they were not desir-able. Innumerable such examples can be given for these. For example, laxatives which were prescribed at periodic intervals to all for cleaning the alimentary tract are now no longer used unless it is needed for surgery or radiography. At one time in-fection with malarial parasites was therapy for syphilis, etc. Once evidence to the contrary came up or less harmful meth-ods of treatment or more efficient drugs were discovered, the older were discarded and consigned to the dustbins of history. Methods of diagnosis and treatment are not based on some individual's idiosyncrasies but on methods of science. This system absorbed many things from other systems of medicine and knowledge grew.

The so-called 'alternative systems of medicine', many of which cannot be called medicine by any stretch of the most fertile of imaginations, are based on hypotheses unsupported by any evidence.

On the contrary the so-called 'alternative systems of medicine', many of which cannot be called medicine by any stretch of the most fertile of imaginations, are based on hypotheses unsupported by any evidence. They are based on presumptions of certain individuals, pseudoscientific assumptions and unsupported claims. They also peddle unproven remedies, devices and books of dubious claims. There are arguments that these are very inexpensive, but the facts prove otherwise. In quack 'therapies' like aroma 'therapy' small phials of perfumes are sold at exorbitant prices. While one may claim that there are more expensive perfumes that are no problem, if a perfume is sold as such. One can decide whether one wants to purchase them at the quoted price. But, when it is claimed as a curative, evidence is needed, which is never forthcoming. Most of the time the so-called evidence offered by these proclaimers of alternative medicine are testimonials from well-known individuals, and are nothing more than anecdotal.

Legal Status of Alternative Medicine

Many countries have very effective laws to deal with these so-called alternative systems. If anyone claims that their concoction, device or incantation can be used as treatment for any disease, it is up to them to show scientific studies as proof. The governments in these countries also have rigorous testing standards. If one fails they are subjected to heavy penalties including imprisonment. This is why many peddlers of such nonsense are limited in their activities in these countries. Some of the Indian peddlers of such concoctions remain silent about their claims in such countries, but some of them pitch their products calling them nutritional supplements made from edible ingredients! Some of them cannot be sold as such either, because of the unacceptable levels of toxic metals and such! But, in our country these people are lucky, though there are laws such as the Consumer Protection Act, the section under unfair trade practices of the MRTP Act and the Drugs and Magic Remedies (Objectionable Advertisements) Act. The peddlers of these dubious concoctions and quack remedies manage to get away through various loopholes such as claiming them to be traditional remedies, or under religious freedom, etc. Sometimes the advertisements are so cleverly worded that it is very difficult to pin them down. Under many of these only the affected parties can complain or go in for litigation, which they are loath to. These are so rampant that even a Supreme Court judgment has not affected them. In 2004 the Supreme Court of India passed judgment on more than a dozen so-called systems of medicine, stating that they have absolutely no scientific basis and should not be allowed to be practiced as systems of medicine. These include, in addition to those already mentioned above, things like magneto therapy, gem therapy, color therapy, urine therapy, etc.

The Supreme Court of India passed judgment on more than a dozen so-called systems of medicine, stating that they have absolutely no scientific basis and should not be allowed to be practiced.

Again the term 'therapy' is a very vague term! So, a hotel could call itself as an Institute of Nutritional Therapy. There are some calling themselves Naturopathic Hospitals and the practitioners as Naturopathic Doctors. If nature itself can heal, why are these so-called therapists needed?! One can get a certificate for many of these quack therapies from degree mills offering these and then call themselves as therapists and add prefix Dr. to their names! I can always say that I am under treatment for breatho therapy and every day get my therapy from the Institute of Nutritional Sciences round the corner (of course a fancy name for a restaurant!). A barber could call himself a Tonsorial Therapist (the surgeons used to be those long back and that is why the surgeons have the title Mr. in England!) and so on.

How do these alternative therapies gain legitimacy? One reason is their ads and programs on TV channels. We can see many of these so-called specialists on TV channels—the cancerologists, the kidneyologists, the sexologists and so on. Of course the terminologies I have used for these so-called specialists are deliberate, as the respective specializations are called different names among the properly qualified practitioners. Then we have people with respectable qualifications endorsing such quacks. Once I remember a professor of medicine who was also the dean of a medical college inaugurating the asthma relief camp of a steroid quack. The very same person who went on to become the vice chancellor of a deemed university also presided over a convocation of a quack and handed over degrees to other quacks. The quack who was the leader was hounded out of Mangalore and is now pursuing his quackery at Kolhapur, I am told! Some of the qualified people treat patients referred to them by such, treating them as if they are their professional colleagues. One thing that has to be admired about these alternative medicine guys is their gift of the gab! Their bedside manners and their use of pseudoscientific jargon could put any genuine specialist to shame! Their easy accessibility and their flexible terms of payment, money-back guarantee and such attractive qualities are another plus point.

Why Scientific Medicine Is Better than Alternatives

For those who are very fond of alternatives of our ancient civilization—want an alternative mobile phone? Breed homing pigeons and carry them in your pocket! You can send home messages in your alternative mobile. Want an alternative idiot box? Take a cardboard box of the size you want and go to the performance you want to see—open it, hold it in front of your face and you have an alternative TV with full stereo hi-fi audio! Want an alternative car? Go to our villages where you have the all-terrain one or two ox-power models! I am sure even the most vehement supporters of so-called 'alternative medicine' would not choose these!

Why does this so-called 'alternative medicine' work sometimes? As any honest general practitioner will tell you 80% of the patients have some self-limiting disorder! These patients will get cured whether any treatment is administered or not! It is the main task of the family doctor to decide whether you need specialist treatment or not. This doctor also prescribes palliatives so that the symptoms become manageable.

So, that raises the question as to how safe is it to go to these quacks? One has to remember that without proper training these people are in no position to determine which disease/ condition falls in which category. Again, they refuse to admit failure and go on administering different things about which they have little knowledge and/or training. Some diseases that can be cured in the starting stages become untreatable later, like cancer for example. Some emergencies require immediate treatment—conditions such as acute abdominal pain, internal bleeding, etc.

Remember, there are no alternative lives and there is no alternative to good health. Keep this in mind when you think of something like alternative medicine. Again, keep in mind that a color therapist will not go to a gem therapist when he is ill! He will go to the nearest qualified specialist in scientific medicine with all the latest gadgets and drugs! To hell with the alternative treatments! As a wag remarked, let us see a music therapist treat an aroma therapist or vice versa!

Despite all the shortcomings that can be blamed on evidence-based, scientific medicine—it works better than pseudoscientific 'treatments', and it is based on sound evidence and peer-reviewed scientific studies. It is not based on any one individual's untested hypothesis or divine revelations or testimonies of individuals. It changes as new findings emerge, always subject to self-criticism and peer review. In fact, most published scientific work is comprised of reviews of past methods. More importantly science-based medicine changes and does not crow about the good old times when everything was so good and everyone was so healthy. It does not have any unquestionable central dogma.

Promotion of Complementary and Alternative Therapies Is Deceptive

Marilynn Marchione

Marilynn Marchione is a prize-winning medical writer for the Associated Press.

At one of the nation's top trauma hospitals, a nurse circles a patient's bed, humming and waving her arms as if shooing evil spirits. Another woman rubs a quartz bowl with a wand, making tunes that mix with the beeping monitors and hissing respirator keeping the man alive.

They are doing Reiki therapy, which claims to heal through invisible energy fields. The anesthesia chief, Dr. Richard Dutton, calls it "mystical mumbo jumbo." Still, he's a fan.

"It's self-hypnosis" that can help patients relax, he said. "If you tell yourself you have less pain, you actually do have less pain."

Alternative medicine has become mainstream. It is finding wider acceptance by doctors, insurers and hospitals like the shock trauma center at the University of Maryland Medical Center. Consumer spending on it in some cases rivals that of traditional health care.

People turn to unconventional therapies and herbal remedies for everything from hot flashes and trouble sleeping to cancer and heart disease. They crave more "care" in their health care. They distrust drug companies and the government. They want natural, safer remedies.

But often, that is not what they get. Government actions and powerful interest groups have left consumers vulnerable to flawed products and misleading marketing.

Dietary supplements do not have to be proved safe or effective before they can be sold. Some contain natural things you might not want, such as lead and arsenic. Some interfere with other things you may be taking, such as birth control pills.

"Herbals are medicines," with good and bad effects, said Bruce Silverglade of the consumer group Center for Science in the Public Interest.

Government actions and powerful interest groups have left consumers vulnerable to flawed products and misleading marketing.

Contrary to their little-guy image, many of these products are made by big businesses. Ingredients and their countries of origin are a mystery to consumers. They are marketed in ways that manipulate emotions, just like ads for hot cars and cool clothes. Some make claims that average people can't parse as proof of effectiveness or blather, like "restores cell-to-cell communication."

Even therapies that may help certain conditions, such as acupuncture, are being touted for uses beyond their evidence.

An Associated Press review of dozens of studies and interviews with more than 100 sources found an underground medical system operating in plain sight, with a different standard than the rest of medical care, and millions of people using it on blind faith.

How did things get this way?

Widening Use of Alternative Therapies

Fifteen years ago, Congress decided to allow dietary and herbal supplements to be sold without federal Food and Drug Administration [FDA] approval. The number of products soared, from about 4,000 then to well over 40,000 now.

Some [hospitals] offer treatments with little or no scientific basis, to patients who are emotionally vulnerable and gravely ill.

Ten years ago, Congress created a new federal agency to study supplements and unconventional therapies. But more than $2.5 billion of tax-financed research has not found any cures or major treatment advances, aside from certain uses for acupuncture and ginger for chemotherapy-related nausea. If anything, evidence has mounted that many of these pills and therapies lack value.

Yet they are finding ever-wider use:

- Big hospitals and clinics increasingly offer alternative therapies. Many just offer stress reducers like meditation, yoga and massage. But some offer treatments with little or no scientific basis, to patients who are emotionally vulnerable and gravely ill. The Baltimore hospital, for example, is not charging for Reiki but wants to if it can be shown to help. Other hospitals earn fees from treatments such as acupuncture, which insurance does not always cover if the purpose is not sufficiently proven. The giant HMO Kaiser Permanente pays for members to go to a Portland, Ore., doctor who prescribes ayurvedics—traditional herbal remedies from India.

- Some medical schools are teaching future doctors about alternative medicine, sometimes with federal grants. The goal is educating them about what patients are using so they can give evidence-based, nonjudgmental care. But some schools have ties to alternative medicine practitioners and advocates. A University of Minnesota program lets students study nontraditional healing methods at a center in Hawaii supported by a philanthropist fan of such care, though students pay their own travel and living expenses. A private foundation that wants wider inclusion of nontraditional methods sponsors fellowships for hands-on experience at the University of Arizona's [Center for] Integrative Medicine, headed by well-known advocate Dr. Andrew Weil.

- Health insurers are cutting deals to let alternative medicine providers market supplements and services directly to members. At least one insurer promotes these to members with a discount, perhaps leaving an incorrect impression they are covered services and medically sound. Some insurers steer patients to Internet sellers of supplements, even though patients must pay for these out of pocket. There are networks of alternative medicine providers that contract with big employers, just like HMOs.

A few herbal supplements can directly threaten health. A surprising number do not supply what their labels claim, contain potentially harmful substances like lead, or are laced with hidden versions of prescription drugs.

"In testing, one out of four supplements has a problem," said Dr. Tod Cooperman, president of ConsumerLab.com, an independent company that rates such products.

Even when the ingredients aren't risky, spending money for a product with no proven benefit is no small harm when the economy is bad and people can't afford health insurance or healthy food.

But sometimes the cost is far greater. Cancer patients can lose their only chance of beating the disease by gambling on unproven treatments. People with clogged arteries can suffer a heart attack. Children can be harmed by unproven therapies forced on them by parents who distrust conventional medicine.

Mainstream medicine and prescription drugs have problems, too. Popular drugs such as the painkillers Vioxx and Bextra have been pulled from the market after serious side effects emerged once they were widely used by consumers. But at least there are regulatory systems, guideline-setting groups and watchdog agencies helping to keep traditional medicine in line.

The safety net for alternative medicine is far flimsier.

Lack of Regulation

The latest government survey shows the magnitude of risk: More than a third of Americans uses unconventional therapies, including acupuncture, homeopathy, chiropractic, and native or traditional healing methods. These practitioners are largely self-policing, with their own schools and accreditation groups. Some states license certain types, like acupuncturists; others do not.

Tens of millions of Americans take dietary supplements—vitamins, minerals and herbs, ranging from ginseng and selenium to fish oil and zinc, said Steven Mister, president of the Council for Responsible Nutrition, an industry trade group.

"We bristle when people talk about us as if we're just fringe," he said. Supplements are "an insurance policy" if someone doesn't always eat right, he said.

In fact, some are widely recommended by doctors—prenatal vitamins for pregnant women, calcium for older women at risk of osteoporosis, and fish oil for some heart patients, for example. These uses are generally thought to be safe, although independent testing has found quality problems and occasional safety concerns with specific products, such as too much or too little of a vitamin.

Some studies suggest that vitamin deficiencies can raise the risk of disease. But it is not clear that taking supplements will fix that, and research has found hints of harm, said Dr. Jeffrey White, complementary and alternative medicine chief at the National Cancer Institute. A doctor with a big interest in nutrition, he sees the field as "an area of opportunity" that deserves serious study.

So does Dr. Josephine Briggs, director of the National Center for Complementary and Alternative Medicine, the federal agency Congress created a decade ago.

"Most patients are not treated very satisfactorily," Briggs said. "If we had highly effective, satisfactory conventional treatment we probably wouldn't have as much need for these other strategies and as much public interest in them."

Even critics of alternative medicine providers understand their appeal.

"They give you a lot of time. They treat you like someone special," said R. Barker Bausell, a University of Maryland biostatistician who wrote *Snake Oil Science*, a book about flawed research in the field.

That is why Dr. Mitchell Gaynor, a cancer specialist at the Weill Cornell Medical Center in New York, said he includes nutrition testing and counseling, meditation and relaxation techniques in his treatment, though not everyone would agree with some of the things he recommends.

"You do have people who will say 'chemotherapy is just poison,'" said Gaynor, who tells them he doesn't agree. He'll say: "Cancer takes decades to develop, so you're not going to be able to think that all of a sudden you're going to change your diet or do meditation (and cure it). You need to treat it medically. You can still do things to make your diet better. You can still do meditation to reduce your stress."

Once their fears and feelings are acknowledged, most patients "will do the right thing, do everything they can to save their life," Gaynor said.

Many people buy supplements to treat life's little miseries—trouble falling asleep, menopausal hot flashes, memory lapses, the need to lose weight, sexual problems.

The Dietary Supplement Health and Education Act of 1994 exempted such products from needing FDA approval or proof of safety or effectiveness before they go on sale. "That has resulted in consumers wasting billions of dollars on products of either no or dubious benefit," said Silverglade of the public interest group.

Many hope that President Barack Obama's administration will take a new look. In the meantime, some outlandish claims are drawing a backlash. The industry has stepped up self-policing—the Council for Responsible Nutrition hired a lawyer to work with the Council of Better Business Bureaus and file complaints against problem sellers.

People need to keep a healthy skepticism about that magical marketing term "natural."

"We certainly don't think this is a huge problem in the industry," Mister said, but he acknowledges occasionally seeing infomercials "that promise the world."

"The outliers were making the public feel that this entire industry was just snake oil and that there weren't any legitimate products," said Andrea Levine, ad division chief for the business bureaus.

The FDA just issued its first guidelines for good manufacturing practices, aimed at improving supplement safety. Consumer groups say the rules don't go far enough—for example, they don't set limits on contaminants like lead and arsenic—but they do give the FDA more leverage after problems come to light.

The Federal Trade Commission is filing more complaints about deceptive marketing. One of the largest settlements occurred last August [2008]—$30 million from the makers of Airborne, a product marketed with a folksy "invented by a teacher" slogan that claimed to ward off germs spread through the air.

People need to keep a healthy skepticism about that magical marketing term "natural," said Kathy Allen, a dietitian at Moffitt Cancer Center in Tampa.

The truth is, supplements lack proof of safety or benefit. Asked to take a drug under those terms, "most of us would say 'no,'" Allen said. "When it says 'natural,' the perception is there is no harm. And that is just not true."

CHAPTER 2

Are the Major Alternatives to Conventional Medicine Safe and Effective?

Chapter Preface

The forms of alternative medicine discussed in this chapter all are complete systems that some people use *instead of* conventional medical care. Some of them have existed for centuries in other cultures and are still predominant there. Others developed more recently, in the nineteenth century, before what is now known as conventional medicine was as firmly established as it is today. What these systems have in common is that they are based on a different philosophy from that underlying modern scientific medicine, and their practitioners are trained differently. Their adherents believe that the human body has the ability to heal itself from illness and that the proper role of health care is to encourage this capability rather than to intervene with drugs and nonemergency surgery. They do not accept the idea that biology alone determines the state of the body; rather, they consider it essential to view the patient—body, mind, and spirit—as a whole person.

Researchers are learning more and more all the time about ways in which state of mind affects biochemical responses initiated by the brain. So it might be thought that conventional and alternative medicines are growing closer together. However, that is not the case, because the alternative systems have their own theories of how the body works that are very different from those of biology. For example, some Eastern systems are based on belief in a form of vital energy called *qi* or *chi* (pronounced "chee") that sustains living things and flows through the body in a way that can become uneven, so that the aim of medical treatment is to correct the imbalance. No such energy is detectable by science, and so scientifically oriented people are apt to view it as mere superstition. Yet healers who were convinced that it exists—traditional acupuncturists, among others—were curing illness long before scientific medicine existed.

How can this be? Opinions on that issue differ widely. Scientists and conventional doctors tend to think that people cured by the application of nonscientific principles were not really very sick in the first place, and would have recovered even if untreated. Alternative therapists and their patients, on the other hand, believe that today's scientific theories are mistaken, or at best incomplete. An intermediate view held by some people is that nonscientific theories of medicine are metaphors—conceptions that are not literally true, but that nevertheless express truth in a symbolic way that may often be useful.

Most alternative healers emphasize that treatment methods should be natural, in contrast to the technologically based drugs and surgery on which modern medicine relies. The focus of these methods on nutrition, supplements, and lifestyle is indeed natural and generally less risky than drug treatment in cases where it is appropriate. However, various forms of alternative medicine also incorporate treatments such a acupuncture, spinal manipulation, and colon hydrotherapy that cannot be considered natural by most people's standards. Furthermore, the fact that herbs grow naturally does not mean that they are all harmless, nor does it mean that they are safer than the drugs of which they are sometimes ingredients. Furthermore, as has often been pointed out, the natural result of many physical conditions is sickness or death. All treatment, under any system of medicine, intervenes in nature to some extent; so whether "natural" is a measure of superiority depends on the particular circumstances.

The five main alternative medical systems most widely known in the United States are traditional Chinese medicine, of which acupuncture is the best-known element; homeopathy, which in the nineteenth century competed with now-conventional medicine for dominance; chiropractic care, which is commonly used for back pain even by patients who don't go to chiropractors for other problems; ayurveda, the traditional medical system of India; and naturopathy, the popularity of which is growing in reaction to impersonal high-tech medicine. A relatively small number of people use one of these systems exclusively, avoiding any contact with conventional medicine.

Today, however, it is more common for treatments derived from alternative medical systems to be used as complementary therapies alongside conventional medicine. Acupuncture is a prime example of this; more and more, Western medical institutions are beginning to offer it. Many people visit both chiropractors and medical doctors on a regular basis, and many favor naturopathy for minor illnesses while turning to conventional medicine for serious ailments. Therefore, although such therapies are often called "alternative," for most Americans they are additions, rather than alternatives, to standard medical care.

Acupuncture Is Suitable for Treating a Wide Range of Conditions

Douglas Dupler, Teresa G. Odle, and David Edward Newton

Douglas Dupler, Teresa G. Odle, and David Edward Newton are writers who specialize in health care communications.

Acupuncture is one of the main forms of treatment in traditional Chinese medicine. It involves the use of sharp, thin needles that are inserted in the body at specific points. This process is believed to adjust and alter the body's energy flow into healthier patterns and is used to treat a wide variety of illnesses and health conditions.

The original text of Chinese medicine is the *Nei Ching, The Yellow Emperor's Classic of Internal Medicine,* which is estimated to be at least 2,500 years old. Thousands of books followed on the subject of Chinese healing, and its basic philosophies spread long ago to other Asian civilizations. Nearly all of the forms of Oriental medicine which are used in the West in the 2000s—including acupuncture, *shiatsu acupressure* massage, and macrobiotics—are part of or have their roots in Chinese medicine. Legend has it that acupuncture developed when early Chinese physicians observed unpredicted effects of puncture wounds in Chinese warriors. The oldest known text on acupuncture, the *Systematic Classic of Acupuncture,* dates back to 282 A.D. Although acupuncture is its best known technique, Chinese medicine traditionally uses herbal remedies, dietary therapy, lifestyle changes, and other means to treat patients.

In the early 1900s, only a few Western physicians who had visited China knew about and used acupuncture. But outside of Asian American communities it remained virtually unknown until the 1970s, when Richard Nixon became the first U.S. president to visit China. On Nixon's trip, journalists were amazed to observe major operations being performed on patients without the use of anesthetics. Instead, fully conscious patients were being operated on with only acupuncture needles inserted into them to control pain. During that time, a famous columnist for the *New York Times*, James Reston, had to undergo surgery and elected to use acupuncture instead of pain medication, and he wrote some convincing stories on its effectiveness.

As of 2008 acupuncture was practiced in all U.S. 50 states by more than 9,000 practitioners, with about 4,000 medical doctors (MDs) including it in their practices.

As of 2008 acupuncture was practiced in all U.S. 50 states by more than 9,000 practitioners, with about 4,000 medical doctors (MDs) including it in their practices. Acupuncture has shown notable success in treating many conditions, and more than 15 million Americans have used it as a therapy. Acupuncture, however, remains largely unsupported by the medical establishment. The American Medical Association has been resistant to encouraging research, as the practice is based on concepts markedly unlike the Western scientific model.

Several forms of acupuncture are being used as of 2008 in the United States. Japanese acupuncture uses extremely thin needles and does not incorporate herbal medicine in its practice. Auricular acupuncture uses acupuncture points only on the ear, which are believed to stimulate and balance internal organs. In France, where acupuncture is very popular and more widely accepted by the medical establishment, neurologist Paul Nogier developed a system of acupuncture based on neuroendocrine theory rather than on traditional Chinese concepts, which has gained some use in the United States.

Benefits of Acupuncture

The World Health Organization (WHO) recommends acupuncture as an effective treatment for over forty medical problems, including allergies; respiratory conditions; gastrointestinal disorders; gynecological problems; nervous conditions; disorders of the eyes, nose and throat; and childhood illnesses, among others. Acupuncture has been used in the treatment of alcoholism and substance abuse. In 2002, a center in Maine received a unique grant to study acupuncture treatment for substance abuse. Although recognizing that acupuncture had been used before for helping those with abuse problems, this study sought to show that ear acupuncture's effects on relaxation response helped those abusing drugs and alcohol better deal with the anxiety and life circumstances thought to lead them to substance abuse.

The World Health Organization (WHO) recommends acupuncture as an effective treatment for over forty medical problems.

Acupuncture is an effective and low-cost treatment for headaches and chronic pain, associated with problems like back injuries and arthritis. It has also been used to supplement invasive Western treatments such as chemotherapy and surgery. Acupuncture is generally more effective when used as prevention or before a health condition becomes acute, but it has been used to help patients suffering from cancer and AIDS. In 2002, the National Institutes of Health announced that pain from certain musculoskeletal conditions such as fibromyalgia could be helped by acupuncture. Acupuncture has limited value in treating conditions or traumas that require surgery or emergency care (such as for broken bones).

Basic Ideas of Chinese Medicine

Chinese medicine views the body as a small part of the universe and subject to universal laws and principles of harmony and balance. Chinese medicine does not draw a sharp line, as Western medicine does, between mind and body. The Chinese system believes that emotions and mental states are every bit as influential on disease as purely physical mechanisms and considers factors such as work, environment, lifestyle, and relationships as fundamental to the overall picture of a patient's health. Chinese medicine also uses very different symbols and ideas to discuss the body and health. While Western medicine typically describes health in terms of measurable physical processes made up of chemical reactions, the Chinese use the ideas of yin and yang, chi, the organ system, and the five elements to describe health and the body. To understand the ideas behind acupuncture, it is worthwhile to introduce some of these basic terms.

Chinese medicine does not draw a sharp line, as Western medicine does, between mind and body.

YIN AND YANG. According to Chinese philosophy, the universe and the body can be described by two separate but complementary principles, that of yin and yang. For example, in temperature, yin is cold and yang is hot. In gender, yin is female and yang is male. In activity, yin is passive and yang is active. In light, yin is dark and yang is bright. In direction, yin is inward and downward and yang is outward and up, and so on. Nothing is ever completely yin or yang, but a combination of the two. These two principles are always interacting, opposing, and influencing each other. The goal of Chinese medicine is not to eliminate either yin or yang, but to allow the two to balance each other and exist harmoniously together. For instance, if a person suffers from symptoms of high blood pressure, the Chinese system would say that the heart organ might have too much yang and would recommend methods either to reduce the yang or to increase the yin of the heart, depending on the other symptoms and organs in the body. Thus, acupuncture therapies seek to either increase or reduce yang or increase or reduce yin in particular regions of the body.

CHI. Another fundamental concept of Chinese medicine is that of chi (pronounced *chee,* also spelled *qi*). Chi is the fundamental life energy of the universe. It is invisible and is found in the environment in air, water, food, and sunlight. In the body, it is the invisible vital force that creates and animates life. Humans are all born with inherited amounts of chi, and they also get acquired chi from the food they eat and the air they breathe. The level and quality of a person's chi also depends on the state of physical, mental, and emotional balance. Chi travels through the body along channels called *meridians.*

THE ORGAN SYSTEM. In the Chinese system, there are twelve main organs: the lung, large intestine, stomach, spleen, heart, small intestine, urinary bladder, kidney, liver, gallbladder, pericardium, and the "triple warmer," which represents the entire torso region. Each organ has chi energy associated with it, and each organ interacts with particular emotions on the mental level. As there are twelve organs, there are twelve types of chi that can move through the body, and these move through twelve main channels or meridians. Chinese doctors connect symptoms to organs. That is, symptoms are caused by yin/yang imbalances in one or more organs or by an unhealthy flow of chi to or from one organ to another. Each organ has a different profile of symptoms it can manifest.

THE FIVE ELEMENTS. Another basis of Chinese theory is that the world and body are made up of five main elements: wood, fire, earth, metal, and water. These elements are all interconnected, and each element either generates or controls another element. For instance, water controls fire, and earth generates metal. Each organ is associated with one of the five elements. The Chinese system uses elements and organs to describe and treat conditions. For instance, the kidney is associated with water, and the heart is associated with fire, and the two organs are related as water and fire are related. If the kidney is weak, then there might be a corresponding fire problem in the heart, so treatment might be made by acupuncture or herbs to cool the heart system and/or increase energy in the kidney system.

In Chinese medicine . . . the goal of any remedy or treatment is to assist the body in reestablishing its innate harmony.

The Chinese have developed an intricate system that describes how organs and elements are related to physical and mental symptoms, and the above example is a simple one. Although this system sounds suspect to Western scientists, some interesting parallels have been observed. For instance, Western medicine has observed that with severe heart problems, kidney failure often follows, but it still does not know exactly why. In Chinese medicine, this connection between the two organs has long been established.

MEDICAL PROBLEMS AND ACUPUNCTURE. In Chinese medicine, disease is seen as imbalances in the organ system or chi meridians, and the goal of any remedy or treatment is to assist the body in reestablishing its innate harmony. Disease can be caused by internal factors such as emotions, external factors such as the environment and weather, and other factors such as injuries, trauma, diet, and germs. However, infection is seen not as primarily a problem with germs and viruses but as a weakness in the energy of the body that is allowing a sickness to occur. In Chinese medicine, no two illnesses are ever the same, as each body has its own characteristics of symptoms and balance. Acupuncture is used to open or adjust the flow of chi throughout the organ system, which will strengthen the body and prompt it to heal itself.

A Visit to the Acupuncturist

Typically, an acupuncturist first gets a thorough idea of a patient's medical history and symptoms, both physical and emotional, using a questionnaire and interview. Then the acupuncturist examines the patient to find further symptoms, looking closely at the tongue, the pulse at various points in the body, the complexion, general behavior, and other signs like coughs or pains. From this examination, the practitioner is able to determine patterns of symptoms that indicate which organs and areas are imbalanced. Depending on the problem, the acupuncturist inserts needles to manipulate chi on one or more of the twelve organ meridians. On these twelve meridians, there are nearly 2,000 points that can be used in acupuncture, with around 200 points being most frequently used by traditional acupuncturists. During an individual treatment, one to 20 needles may be used, depending on which meridian points are chosen.

Acupuncture is generally a safe procedure.

Acupuncture needles are sterilized, and acupuncture is a very safe procedure. The depth of insertion of needles varies, depending on which chi channels are being treated. Some points barely go beyond superficial layers of skin, while some acupuncture points require a depth of 1–3 in (3–8 cm) of needle. The needles generally do not cause pain. Patients sometimes report pinching sensations and often pleasant sensations as the body experiences healing. Depending on the problem, the acupuncturist might spin or move the needles, or even pass a slight electrical current through some of them. *Moxibustion* may sometimes be used. Moxibustion is a process in which an herbal mixture (moxa or *mugwort*) is either burned like incense on the acupuncture point or on the end of the needle, a process believed to stimulate chi in a particular way. Also, acupuncturists sometimes use *cupping*, during which small suction cups are placed on meridian points to stimulate them.

How long the needles are inserted also varies. Some patients require only a quick in and out insertion to clear problems and provide *tonification* (strengthening of health), while some other conditions might require needles inserted up to an hour or more. The average visit to an acupuncturist takes about 30 minutes. The number of visits to the acupuncturist varies, with some conditions improved in one or two sessions and others requiring a series of six or more visits over the course of weeks or months. . . .

Acupuncture is generally a safe procedure. If individuals are in doubt about a medical condition, more than one physician should be consulted. Also, individuals should feel comfortable and confident that their acupuncturist is knowledgeable and properly trained.

Mainstream medicine has been slow to accept acupuncture.

Research and General Acceptance

Mainstream medicine has been slow to accept acupuncture. Although more medical doctors are using the technique, the American Medical Association does not recognize it as a specialty. The reason for this position is that the mechanism of acupuncture is difficult to understand or measure scientifically, such as the invisible energy of chi in the body. Western medicine, admitting that acupuncture works in many cases, has theorized that the energy meridians are actually part of the nervous system and that acupuncture relieves pain by releasing endorphins, or natural painkillers, into the bloodstream. Despite the ambiguity in the biochemistry involved, acupuncture continues to show effectiveness in clinical tests, from reducing pain to alleviating the symptoms of chronic illnesses, and in the 2000s research in acupuncture was growing. The National Center for Complementary and Alternative Medicine of the National Institutes of Health funded research in the use of acupuncture on a number of conditions, including depression, attention-deficit disorder, arthritis, and post-traumatic stress disorder.

Medical acupuncture has evolved in the United States in an atmosphere that focuses on traditional Western methods, such as surgical techniques and pain management, and not as part of Chinese medicine overall. Medical acupuncture is performed by an MD or an osteopathic physician (DO). As of 2008, 23 states allowed only this type of acupuncture.

Acupuncture Produces No Greater Effect than a Placebo

Richard Saint Cyr

Richard Saint Cyr is an American doctor who lives in China and practices Western-style family medicine at the International Medical Center in Beijing.

One of my continuing goals in China is to find traditional Chinese medicines and practices that I can integrate into my Western, allopathic-style family practice. As I've reported a few times, I've been struggling to find Chinese herbal medicines that I am comfortable prescribing, usually due to lack of evidence for a clear benefit.

As for acupuncture, there are actually a lot more well-designed studies done on this field when compared to Chinese herbs, mostly because Europe and the West have become very interested over the last couple decades and are funding better clinical trials. The evidence trail is building, which is great for everyone. So, what works, and what doesn't?

The *New York Times* had a very readable article last week [August 2010] which covers this issue. The gist of the article discusses the most recent, well-designed studies on back pains and other disorders; the studies usually show no difference between acupuncture and placebo (usually a "sham" needle that doesn't penetrate the skin). In other words, the best studies lately are usually showing that most of the perceived effect from acupuncture is simply a placebo effect.

These recent findings are by no means surprising, as most of the best studies have been reporting similar conclusions for many years. The best collection of acupuncture research is from the Cochrane review group, which performs the world's most rigorous reviews of all treatments, including alternative medicines. They have an outstanding collection of the best literature on acupuncture which details the best evidence regarding a number of acupuncture treatments. Unfortunately, as many other researchers have noted, the only treatments for which acupuncture is even mildly effective are for musculoskeletal problems and nausea. There is some evidence of effectiveness for treatments for IVF [in vitro fertilization], as well as insomnia. But many well-designed studies have specifically shown no benefit over placebo for a host of other treatments. The Cochrane group also commonly finds that the quality of studies is very poor and cannot recommend either for or against.

The only treatments for which acupuncture is even mildly effective are for musculoskeletal problems and nausea.

There Is Little Evidence That Acupuncture Is Effective

Readers should be aware that this is not simply a Western bias against alternative medicines; in April a group from Beijing Hospital published in a Chinese journal a similar literature review of acupuncture for insomnia, and couldn't even make a conclusion because the studies were so poor:

> Regarding the assessment of the therapeutic effect, measuring scales are often adopted in overseas studies, while in domestic researches, self-drawn standards are frequently used. In conclusion, there have [been] no high-quality clinical trials about acupuncture treatment of primary insomnia in China at the present, and the related evaluating methods could not definitely confirm the efficacy of acupuncture in relieving insomnia. Therefore, a strict and scientific clinical trial scheme being in line with evidence-based medicine is urgently needed in the coming studies on acupuncture treatment of primary insomnia.

The Cochrane's reports cover a lot of therapies that I'm sure many readers have tried. Here's an example of Cochrane's findings on the most common acupuncture treatment—low-back pain:

> There is insufficient evidence to make any recommendations about acupuncture or dry-needling for acute low-back pain. For chronic low-back pain, results show that acupuncture is more effective for pain relief than no treatment or sham treatment, in measurements taken up to three months. The results also show that for chronic low-back pain, acupuncture is more effective for improving function than no treatment, in the short term. Acupuncture is not more effective than other conventional and "alternative" treatments. When acupuncture is added to other conventional therapies, it relieves pain and improves function better than the conventional therapies alone. However, effects are only small. Dry-needling appears to be a useful adjunct to other therapies for chronic low-back pain.

For depression:

> "... Thirty trials, and 2812 participants were included in the review and meta-analysis, however there was insufficient evidence that acupuncture can assist with the management of depression."

For migraines:

> In the four trials in which acupuncture was compared to a proven prophylactic drug treatment, patients receiving acupuncture tended to report more improvement and fewer side effects. Collectively, the studies suggest that migraine patients benefit from acupuncture, although the correct placement of needles seems to be less relevant than is usually thought by acupuncturists.

For insomnia:

> Seven studies were eligible for inclusion in the review, involving 590 participants. The studies were of low method-

ological quality and were diverse in the types of participant, acupuncture treatments and sleep outcome measures used, which limited the ability to pool the findings and draw conclusions. Currently there is a lack of high-quality clinical evidence supporting the treatment of people with insomnia using acupuncture. More rigorous studies are needed to assess the efficacy and safety of various forms of acupuncture for treating people with insomnia.

Other reputable sources of evidence include the National Center for Complementary and Alternative Medicine. Also, the excellent evidence-based blog *The C.A.M. Report* has a section on acupuncture studies. Another blog, *Science-Based Medicine*, has a section on acupuncture. And I've started to read a couple of recently published books which also take a rigorous, evidence-based review of alternative medicines, and I recommend them to my readers. One is called *Trick or Treatment: The Undeniable Facts About Alternative Medicine*; the other is called *Snake Oil Science: The Truth About Complementary and Alternative Medicine*. . . .

One of the problems of relying on alternative medicines (which probably are a placebo effect) would be that you are losing valuable time in getting proper, effective treatment for something which may be serious.

Does It Even Matter What the Science Shows?

Many readers may remark that complementary medicine, even if it is just a placebo effect, is still better than nothing. And I think that's partly true; the placebo effect is simply a person believing and hoping they will get better. It's an amazing and profoundly humbling revelation that simply believing in healing can set off a biochemical cascade which can boost your immune system and help your body to heal itself. The placebo effect is proven time and again in every study ever done. It's called *faith*, and it's crucial in any illness and is crucial just for living. Here's a nice quote from the *New York Times* article:

> . . . acupuncture believers say it doesn't really matter whether Western scientific studies find that the treatment has a strong placebo effect. After all, the goal of what they call integrative medicine, which combines conventional and alternative treatments like acupuncture, is to harness the body's power to heal itself. It doesn't matter whether that power is stimulated by a placebo effect or by skillful placement of needles.

> "In general in integrative medicine, when patients are involved in their healing process, they have a tendency to do better," said Angela Johnson, a practitioner of Chinese medicine at Rush Children's Hospital in Chicago who is conducting a pilot study of acupuncture to relieve pain in children. "I believe that's part of the reason why they get better." . . .

But one of the problems of relying on alternative medicines (which probably are a placebo effect) would be that you are losing valuable time in getting proper, effective treatment for something which may be serious. Also, you will potentially be spending a lot of your personal money for treatments no better than a placebo.

I personally feel that if a patient wants to try acupuncture for musculoskeletal problems like back pains, then they are welcome to try. It's usually very safe, and sometimes can help; it's also an interesting experience to do at least once. For almost all other treatments, I would try to pull up Cochrane database evidence for such treatment and show my patients, and let them make their own decisions.

Hopefully by now, my long-term readers are convinced that *evidence-based medicine* is the most proper method of testing therapies, and that all treatments of any culture's medical systems should be tested and proven with rigorous clinical trials. So, I hope we are all open-minded enough to believe that when the best trials show no benefit for a specific treatment—whether mainstream or alternative—then doctors shouldn't recommend that, and consumers should think twice before wasting their money on it. On the flip side, doctors such as myself should be open-minded and recommend alternative treatments that are proven to work. There just aren't that many . . . yet?

Homeopathic Medicines Are Worthless and Should Not Be Sold as Drugs

Stephen Barrett

Stephen Barrett is a retired psychiatrist who is well known as a medical writer, editor, and consumer advocate strongly opposed to alternative therapies. He has authored many books and operates twenty-four websites including Quackwatch.org.

Homeopathic "remedies" enjoy a unique status in the health marketplace: They are the only category of quack products legally marketable as drugs. This situation is the result of two circumstances. First, the 1938 Federal Food, Drug, and Cosmetic Act, which was shepherded through Congress by a homeopathic physician who was a senator, recognizes as drugs all substances included in the *Homeopathic Pharmacopeia of the United States*. Second, the FDA [Food and Drug Administration] has not held homeopathic products to the same standards as other drugs. Today they are marketed in health-food stores, in pharmacies, in practitioner offices, by multilevel distributors, through the mail, and on the Internet.

Basic Misbeliefs

Samuel Hahnemann (1755–1843), a German physician, began formulating homeopathy's basic principles in the late 1700s. Hahnemann was justifiably distressed about bloodletting, leeching, purging, and other medical procedures of his day that did far more harm than good. Thinking that these treatments were intended to "balance the body's 'humors' by opposite effects," he developed his "law of similars"—a notion that symptoms of disease can be cured by extremely small amounts

Stephen Barrett, "Homeopathy: The Ultimate Fake," Quackwatch.org, August 23, 2009.

of substances that produce similar symptoms in healthy people when administered in large amounts. The word "homeopathy" is derived from the Greek words *homoios* (similar) and *pathos* (suffering or disease).

Hahnemann and his early followers conducted "provings" in which they administered herbs, minerals, and other substances to healthy people, including themselves, and kept detailed records of what they observed. Later these records were compiled into lengthy reference books called *materia medica*, which are used to match a patient's symptoms with a "corresponding" drug.

Hahnemann declared that diseases represent a disturbance in the body's ability to heal itself and that only a small stimulus is needed to begin the healing process. He also claimed that chronic diseases were manifestations of a suppressed itch (*psora*), a kind of miasma or evil spirit. At first he used small doses of accepted medications. But later he used enormous dilutions and theorized that the smaller the dose, the more powerful the effect—a notion commonly referred to as the "law of infinitesimals." That, of course, is just the opposite of the dose-response relationship that pharmacologists have demonstrated. . . .

Because homeopathic remedies were actually less dangerous than those of nineteenth-century medical orthodoxy, many medical practitioners began using them. At the turn of the twentieth century, homeopathy had about 14,000 practitioners and 22 schools in the United States. But as medical science and medical education advanced, homeopathy declined sharply in America, where its schools either closed or converted to modern methods. The last pure homeopathic school in this country closed during the 1920s. . . .

At Best, the "Remedies" Are Placebos

Homeopathic products are made from minerals, botanical substances, and several other sources. If the original substance is soluble, one part is diluted with either nine or ninety-nine parts of distilled water and/or alcohol and shaken vigorously (succussed); if insoluble, it is finely ground and pulverized in similar proportions with powdered lactose (milk sugar). One part of the diluted medicine is then further diluted, and the process is repeated until the desired concentration is reached. Dilutions of 1 to 10 are designated by the Roman numeral X (1X = 1/10, 3X = 1/1,000, 6X = 1/1,000,000). Similarly, dilutions of 1 to 100 are designated by the Roman numeral C (1C = 1/100, 3C = 1/1,000,000, and so on). Most remedies today range from 6X to 30X, but products of 30C or more are marketed.

A 30X dilution means that the original substance has been diluted 1,000,000,000,000,000,000,000,000,000,000 times. Assuming that a cubic centimeter of water contains 15 drops, this number is greater than the number of drops of water that would fill a container more than 50 times the size of the earth. Imagine placing a drop of red dye into such a container so that it disperses evenly. Homeopathy's "law of infinitesimals" is the equivalent of saying that any drop of water subsequently removed from that container will possess an essence of redness. Robert L. Park, Ph.D., a prominent physicist who is executive director of the American Physical Society, has noted that since the least amount of a substance in a solution is one molecule, a 30C solution would have to have at least one molecule of the original substance dissolved in a minimum of 1,000,000,000,000,000,000,000,000,000,000,000, 000,000,000,000,000,000,000,000 molecules of water. This would require a container more than 30,000,000,000 times the size of the earth. . . .

Actually, the laws of chemistry state that there is a limit to the dilution that can be made without losing the original substance altogether. This limit, which is related to Avogadro's number, corresponds to homeopathic potencies of 12C or 24X (1 part in 10^{24}). Hahnemann himself realized that there is virtually no chance that even one molecule of original substance would remain after extreme dilutions. But he believed that the vigorous shaking or pulverizing with each step of dilution leaves behind a "spirit-like" essence—"no longer perceptible to the senses"—which cures by reviving the body's "vital force." Modern proponents assert that even when the last molecule is gone, a "memory" of the substance is retained. This notion is unsubstantiated. Moreover, if it were true, every substance encountered by a molecule of water might imprint an "essence" that could exert powerful (and unpredictable) medicinal effects when ingested by a person.

Many proponents claim that homeopathic products resemble vaccines because both provide a small stimulus that triggers an immune response. This comparison is not valid. The amounts of active ingredients in vaccines are much greater and can be measured. Moreover, immunizations produce antibodies whose concentration in the blood can be measured, but high-dilution homeopathic products produce no measurable response. In addition, vaccines are used preventively, not for curing symptoms. . . .

Since many homeopathic remedies contain no detectable amount of active ingredient, it is impossible to test whether they contain what their labels say.

Unimpressive "Research"

Since many homeopathic remedies contain no detectable amount of active ingredient, it is impossible to test whether they contain what their labels say. Unlike most potent drugs, they have not been proven effective against disease by double-blind clinical testing. In fact, the vast majority of homeopathic products have never even been tested; proponents simply rely on "provings" to tell them what should work.

In 1990, an article in *Review of Epidemiology* analyzed 40 randomized trials that had compared homeopathic treatment with standard treatment, a placebo, or no treatment. The authors concluded that all but three of the trials had major flaws in their design and that only one of those three had reported a positive result. The authors concluded that there is no evidence that homeopathic treatment has any more value than a placebo.

In 1994, the journal *Pediatrics* published an article claiming that homeopathic treatment had been demonstrated to be effective against mild cases of diarrhea among Nicaraguan children. The claim was based on findings that, on certain days, the "treated" group had fewer loose stools than the placebo group. However, [researchers W.] Sampson and [W.] London noted: (1) the study used an unreliable and unproved diagnostic and therapeutic scheme, (2) there was no safeguard against product adulteration, (3) treatment selection was arbitrary, (4) the data were oddly grouped and contained errors and inconsistencies, (5) the results had questionable clinical significance, and (6) there was no public health significance because the only remedy needed for mild childhood diarrhea is adequate fluid intake to prevent or correct dehydration. . . .

Proponents trumpet the few "positive" studies as proof that "homeopathy works." Even if their results can be consistently reproduced (which seems unlikely), the most that the study of a single remedy for a single disease could prove is that the remedy is effective against *that* disease. It would not validate homeopathy's basic theories or prove that homeopathic treatment is useful for other diseases.

Placebo effects can be powerful, of course, but the potential benefit of relieving symptoms with placebos should be weighed against the harm that can result from relying upon—and wasting money on—ineffective products. Spontaneous remission is also a factor in homeopathy's popularity. I believe that most people who credit a homeopathic product for their recovery would have fared equally well without it.

Homeopaths claim to provide care that is safer, gentler, "natural," and less expensive than conventional care—and more concerned with prevention. However, homeopathic treatments prevent nothing, and many homeopathic leaders preach against immunization. Equally bad, a report on the National Center for Homeopathy's 1997 conference described how a homeopathic physician had suggested using homeopathic products to help prevent and treat coronary artery disease. According to the article, the speaker recommended various 30C and 200C products as alternatives to aspirin or cholesterol-lowering drugs, both of which are proven to reduce the incidence of heart attacks and strokes. . . .

The FDA has never recognized any homeopathic remedy as safe and effective for any medical purpose.

Greater Regulation Is Needed

As far as I can tell, the FDA has never recognized any homeopathic remedy as safe and effective for any medical purpose. In 1995, I filed a Freedom of Information Act request that stated:

> I am interested in learning whether the FDA has: (1) received evidence that any homeopathic remedy, now marketed in this country, is effective against any disease or health problem; (2) concluded that any homeopathic product now marketed in the United States is effective against any health problem or condition; (3) concluded that homeopathic remedies are generally effective; or (4) concluded that homeopathic remedies are generally not effective. Please send me copies of all documents in your possession that pertain to these questions.

An official from the FDA Center for Drug Evaluation and Research replied that several dozen homeopathic products were approved many years ago, but these approvals were withdrawn by 1970. In other words, after 1970, no homeopathic remedy had FDA [classification] as "safe and effective" for its intended purpose. As far as I can tell, that statement is still true today.

If the FDA required homeopathic remedies to be proven effective in order to remain marketable—the standard it applies to other categories of drugs—homeopathy would face extinction in the United States. However, there is no indication that the agency is considering this. FDA officials regard homeopathy as relatively benign (compared, for example, to unsubstantiated products marketed for cancer and AIDS) and believe that other problems should get enforcement priority. If the FDA attacks homeopathy too vigorously, its proponents might even persuade a lobby-susceptible Congress to rescue them. Regardless of this risk, the FDA should not permit worthless products to be marketed with claims that they are effective.

Many Patients Are Being Helped by Chiropractic Care

Julie Deardorff

Julie Deardorff is a health columnist for the Chicago Tribune.

Chiropractors are best known for treating back and neck pain. But can their hands-on manipulations of the spine also help with colic, asthma, ear infections, allergies and digestive issues?

Though it's a controversial notion, some chiropractors are aggressively marketing themselves as holistic, primary-care healers who can treat a broad scope of ailments ranging from acid reflux to infertility. Others in the field say chiropractors should focus on musculoskeletal disorders such as back pain, where evidence for efficacy is the strongest.

The internal philosophical divide has given the profession a confusing image, making it difficult for consumers to know when, if ever, they should visit a chiropractor.

"We often hear from chiropractors that 'chiropractic is more than just back pain.' But is it?" Rhode Island chiropractor Donald Murphy asked in a commentary published last year [2008] in the journal *Chiropractic and Osteopathy*. "And more importantly, does it have to be?"

Though conventional practitioners have often scorned them for making unfounded claims, chiropractors are now established as mainstream health-care providers. Many health plans and Medicaid now cover their services, and they regularly care for clients ranging from the chronically ill to professional and Olympic athletes. An estimated 8.6 percent of adults in the U.S. use chiropractic or osteopathic manipulation, according to the National Center for Complementary and Alternative Medicine.

Chiropractors typically apply a sudden force to a region of the spine to help loosen a stiff joint, which they say allows the body's natural healing process to take over. During an initial visit, the chiropractor typically takes a health history and performs a physical exam, focusing on the spine. X-rays may be taken, and spinal "adjustments" may be applied with a patient lying facedown or sideways on a table.

Experts say there is evidence the treatments can lessen lower back pain, even if researchers have yet to figure out exactly why.

A nondrug, nonsurgical approach, the manual treatments can be "a good adjunct to musculoskeletal care," said Dr. Joel Press, medical director of the Spine and Sports Rehabilitation Center at the Rehabilitation Institute of Chicago, which employs two chiropractors.

Though conventional practitioners have often scorned them for making unfounded claims, chiropractors are now established as mainstream health-care providers.

Spinal Hygiene

At Chiro One Wellness Centers, however, spinal adjustments are used to treat a wide variety of ailments seemingly unrelated to the spine. Moreover, anyone is encouraged to come in for regular maintenance to prevent disease from occurring.

"We call it spinal hygiene," said chiropractic physician Ashlin Gasiorowski, clinic director of the Chiro One center in Evanston, one of 38 locations in Illinois and Kentucky.

As many as 180 people a day visit his strip mall–based clinic for quick adjustments. "A lot of our patients are here for wellness."

The Chiro One philosophy stems from a concept of chiropractic manipulation from the late 1800s that many view as unscientific and outdated. The theory holds that the spine is the key to our overall health and that human illnesses arise from "subluxation," a term chiropractors use for misalignment of the spine. That distortion allegedly interferes with the ability of the brain to control the body.

"The premise was and still is that the spine and the nervous system are the master systems which control and coordinate all function in the body," said Chiro One Chief Executive Stuart Bernsen. "If there is interference in the communication between the brain and the spinal cord to their end organs or tissues, then those end organs or tissues cannot function properly."

Only a minority of chiropractors still adhere to the original theories of the spine as a source of ill health.

The subluxations can be caused by physical issues such as falling or repetitive movements, as well as mental and emotional stress, Bernsen said. They "affect the health of your nerves, ligaments, discs and joints, weaken your muscle and alter the energy that flows from your brain and nerves to all parts of your body," the Chiro One promotional literature warns. "Your internal organs may get less blood, even your brain may get less oxygen!"

Chiropractors can help, according to the subluxation theory, by removing the pressure.

Ultimately, Bernsen wants Chiro One to be the dominant provider of chiropractic care so it can "define for the public what [chiropractic medicine] is, how to use it and how to benefit," he said.

"Chiropractic is very ill-defined," Bernsen said. "You can go to five chiropractors and have five different experiences. We want to shift the paradigm of how consumers use a chiropractor."

But only a minority of chiropractors still adhere to the original theories of the spine as a source of ill health. On the other end of the spectrum are chiropractors who use a more modern, evidence-based approach that focuses on the diagnosis, assessment and treatment of musculoskeletal conditions using a variety of techniques, with the exception of prescription drugs and surgery.

"This business of 'all disease stemming from spine,' there's no evidence to support that," said chiropractic physician Jim Winterstein, president of the National University of Health Sciences in Lombard, one of 18 accredited chiropractic schools in the country. "And I'd never suggest the adjustment of spine is the answer to human ailments. It plays a role like exercise and nutrition and lifestyle changes. All are tools."

Winterstein also disputes claims that regular adjustments can help improve overall health, again citing a lack of science.

"We have anecdotal evidence that people seem to get healthier—when you manipulate the spine and affect the nervous system, dramatic things sometimes happen—but that's the most we can say at this point," he said. "I release people [from treatment] when they become symptom-free, and they can come back for regular adjustments, but it's their choice."

Bernsen answers his critics by saying the strongest evidence is "in our patients. Tens of millions of Americans routinely opt for chiropractic care because what they're doing isn't working," he said.

Skokie's Jordan Sims, 72, a regular at Chiro One for four years, would agree. He credits his back and neck adjustments with treating his sciatica and lowering his blood pressure and says his entire body feels better. Now pain-free, he returns for maintenance.

"I need the constant care," he said. "If you go away, you eventually get out of balance."

Chiropractic Spine Manipulation May Do More Harm than Good

J.D. Haines

J.D. Haines is a doctor specializing in family and emergency medicine. He is clinical associate professor of family practice at the University of Oklahoma.

When Kristi Bedenbaugh wanted relief from a bad sinus headache, the 24-year-old former beauty queen and medical office administrator made the mistake of consulting a chiropractor. An autopsy performed on Kristi revealed that the manipulation of her neck had split the inner walls of both vertebral arteries, resulting in a fatal stroke.

The chiropractor's violent twisting of her neck caused the torn arterial walls to balloon and block the blood supply to the posterior portion of her brain. Studies confirmed that the blood clots formed on the two days she received her neck adjustments.

Kristi died in 1993. Four years later, South Carolina's State Board of Chiropractic Examiners fined the chiropractor $1,000 and sentenced him to 12 hours of continuing medical education in the area of neurological disorders and emergency response.

Supporters of chiropractic are quick to claim that cases like this are rare. Try telling that to Kristi's family—no matter how great the odds, the outcome was 100% fatal for her. The real problem is that there are no valid statistics concerning the risk of stroke after neck manipulation. Aside from anecdotal reports like Kristi's and a few surveys, little clinical research has addressed this problem.

J.D. Haines, "Fatal Adjustments: How Chiropractic Kills," *eSkeptic: The Email Newsletter of the Skeptics Society*, Oct 21, 2009. Copyright © 1992–2011 Skeptic and its contributors. All rights reserved. Reproduced by permission.

Two recent studies reveal the tip of the iceberg. In 1992, researchers at the Stanford Stroke Center surveyed 486 California neurologists regarding how many patients they had seen within the previous two years who had suffered a stroke within 24 hours of neck manipulation. One hundred seventy-seven neurologists responded, reporting 55 patients between the ages of 21 and 60. One patient died and 48 were left with permanent neurological impairment.

A review of 116 journal articles published between 1925 and 1997 reported 177 cases of neck injury caused by manipulation. Sixty percent of these cases resulted from injury inflicted by chiropractors.

The claim that over 90 different medical illnesses may be successfully treated by spinal manipulation is without any scientific evidence.

Risks Outweigh Benefits

The real tragedy is that cervical spine manipulation is totally worthless in treating problems like Kristi Bedenbaugh's. So, however rare the incidence of adverse outcome, the risk always outweighs any perceived benefit. There is no medically proven benefit whatsoever to chiropractic manipulation of the cervical spine.

While it may be argued that chiropractic is helpful for some cases of low-back pain, the claim that over 90 different medical illnesses may be successfully treated by spinal manipulation is without any scientific evidence. *The Medical Letter on Drugs and Therapeutics* stated on May 27, 2002, "For neck and low-back pain, trials have not demonstrated an unequivocal benefit of chiropractic spinal manipulation over physical therapy and education." The report continues: "Repeated reports of arterial dissection and stroke associated with cervical spine manipulation and cauda equina syndrome associated with manipulation of the lower back suggest a cause and effect relationship."

The report concludes, "Spinal manipulation can cause life-threatening complications. Manipulation of the cervical spine, which has been associated with dissection of the vertebral artery, appears to be especially dangerous."

The major problem with chiropractic is that it was founded upon the false premise that correction of vertebral subluxations will restore and maintain health. Chiropractic philosophy maintains that disease or abnormal function is caused by interference with nerve transmission due to pressure, strain, or tension upon the spinal nerves due to deviation or subluxation within the vertebral column.

Ridiculous Claims

Daniel David Palmer, a tradesman who posed as a magnetic healer, discovered chiropractic in 1895. Palmer's first patient was a deaf janitor who had his hearing restored after Palmer adjusted a bump on his spine. According to Dr. Edmund Crelin, "Magnetic healing was a popular form of quackery in the 19th century in which the healers believed that their personal magnetism was so great that it gave them the power to cure diseases." Palmer summarized his new science:

> I am the originator, the Fountain Head of the essential principle that disease is the result of too much or not enough funtionating [sic]. I created the art of adjusting vertebrae, using the spinous and transverse processes as levers, and named the mental act of accumulating knowledge, the cumulative function, corresponding to the vegetative function—growth of intellectual and physical—together, with the science, art and philosophy—Chiropractic. It was I who combined the science and art and developed the principles thereof. I have answered the question—what is life?

Palmer's egotistical and ridiculous claims are familiar to those who have studied leaders of religious cults. Incredibly, Palmer's philosophy remains the basis of modern-day chiropractic thinking. Palmer's claim that chiropractic answers the question, "What is life?" would be laughable if not for a gullible public who readily accept quackery.

The public is led to believe that physicians disparage chiropractors out of some sort of professional jealousy. Yet there is only one reason that physicians judge chiropractors so harshly. Medicine is scientifically based, whereas chiropractic is not supported by a single legitimate scientific study.

Chiropractors are notorious for performing unnecessary X-rays and so-called maintenance care that often corresponds to the duration of the patient's insurance coverage.

In the first experimental study of the basis of chiropractic's subluxation theory, Dr. Edmund S. Crelin, then an anatomy professor at Yale University, demonstrated that chiropractic theory was erroneous. As retired chiropractor Samuel Homola writes, "Using dissected spines with ligaments attached and the spinal nerves exposed, he used a drill press to bend and twist the spine. Using an ohm meter to record any contact between wired spinal nerves and the foraminal openings, he found that vertebrae could not be displaced enough to stretch or impinge a spinal nerve unless the force was great enough to break the spine. Crelin concluded, 'This experimental study demonstrates conclusively that the subluxation of a vertebrae as defined by chiropractic—the exertion of pressure on a spinal nerve which by interfering with the planned expression of Innate Intelligence produces pathology—does not occur.'"

Physicians have long recognized that spinal nerves are commonly pinched by bony spurs and herniated discs, resulting in musculoskeletal symptoms, without any effect on visceral function, as claimed by chiropractic. Chiropractic theory ignores that the autonomic nervous system maintains the function of the body's organs, even in spinal cord lesions.

Chiropractors are notorious for performing unnecessary X-rays and so-called maintenance care that often corresponds to the duration of the patient's insurance coverage. The greatest threat of chiropractic, however, may be to infants and children. As Homola explains, "Parents are lured by claims that spinal adjustments at an early age can prevent the development of disease and that vaccination may not be necessary." There remains no medical or scientific basis for the treatment of infants and children. A more subtle danger represented by chiropractic is the campaign for public acceptance as primary care providers. The clinical training received by chiropractic students is greatly inferior to that of medical students and residents.

As practiced today, chiropractic is a threat to public health.

Slick Marketing

In today's climate of government-sanctioned alternative therapies, the ignorant consumer may be fooled by slick marketing to believe that chiropractors are qualified to treat a broad range of diseases. As alternative medicine gains wider acceptance, public health will surely suffer. Stephen Barrett, MD, has written that the real enemy of chiropractors is themselves:

> Your basic enemy is yourself. Your colleagues engaged in unscientific practices, economic rip-offs, cheating insurance companies, selling unnecessary supplements and generally overselling themselves. Most chiropractors would like to believe that the number of such colleagues is small. I think it is large and may even be a majority.

As far back as 1924 essayist H.L. Mencken recognized chiropractors as quacks:

> Today the backwoods swarm with chiropractors, and in most States they have been able to exert enough pressure on the rural politicians to get themselves licensed. Any lout with strong hands and arms is perfectly equipped to become a chiropractor. No education beyond the elements is necessary. The takings are often high, and so the profession has attracted thousands of recruits—retired baseball players, work-weary plumbers, truck-drivers, longshoremen, bogus dentists, dubious preachers, cashiered school superintendents. Now and then a quack of some other school—say homeopathy—plunges into it. Hundreds of promising students come from the intellectual ranks of hospital orderlies.

As practiced today, chiropractic is a threat to public health. In an age where phenomenal medical discoveries have improved the health and extended average longevity to almost 80 years, chiropractic remains a holdover from the days of the snake oil salesmen. Every year trusting and naïve Americans suffer needless injury and death due to dangerous cervical spine manipulation. The investigation of the true frequency of complications from chiropractic is a duty that public health officials have long neglected and should undertake at once.

Ayurveda Is a Widely Used Traditional System of Healing

National Center for Complementary and Alternative Medicine

The National Center for Complementary and Alternative Medicine (NCCAM), which is part of the US Department of Health and Human Services, is the federal government's lead agency for scientific research on health care practices that are not generally considered part of conventional medicine.

Ayurvedic medicine (also called Ayurveda) is one of the world's oldest medical systems. It originated in India and has evolved there over thousands of years. In the United States, Ayurvedic medicine is considered complementary and alternative medicine (CAM)—more specifically, a CAM whole medical system. Many therapies used in Ayurvedic medicine are also used on their own as CAM—for example, herbs, massage, and specialized diets. . . .

Ayurvedic medicine, also called Ayurveda, originated in India several thousand years ago. The term "Ayurveda" combines the Sanskrit words *ayur* (life) and *veda* (science or knowledge). Thus, Ayurveda means "the science of life."

In the United States, Ayurvedic medicine is considered a type of CAM and a whole medical system. As with other such systems, it is based on theories of health and illness and on ways to prevent, manage, or treat health problems.

Ayurvedic medicine aims to integrate and balance the body, mind, and spirit; thus, some view it as "holistic." This balance is believed to lead to happiness and health, and to help prevent illness. Ayurvedic medicine also treats specific physical and mental health problems. A chief aim of Ayurvedic

"Ayurvedic Medicine: An Introduction," National Center for Complementary and Alternative Medicine, July 2009.

practices is to cleanse the body of substances that can cause disease, thus helping to reestablish harmony and balance.

Ayurvedic medicine, as practiced in India, is one of the oldest systems of medicine in the world. Many Ayurvedic practices predate written records and were handed down by word of mouth. Two ancient books, written in Sanskrit more than 2,000 years ago, are considered the main texts on Ayurvedic medicine—*Caraka Samhita* and *Sushruta Samhita*. . . .

According to the 2007 National Health Interview Survey, which included a comprehensive survey of CAM use by Americans, more than 200,000 U.S. adults used Ayurvedic medicine in the previous year.

Ayurvedic medicine aims to integrate and balance the body, mind, and spirit.

Underlying Concepts

Ayurvedic medicine has several key foundations that pertain to health and disease. These concepts have to do with universal interconnectedness, the body's constitution (*prakriti*), and life forces (*doshas*).

Interconnectedness. Ideas about the relationships among people, their health, and the universe form the basis for how Ayurvedic practitioners think about problems that affect health. Ayurvedic medicine holds that:

- All things in the universe (both living and nonliving) are joined together.

- Every human being contains elements that can be found in the universe.

- Health will be good if one's mind and body are in harmony, and one's interaction with the universe is natural and wholesome.

- Disease arises when a person is out of harmony with the universe. Disruptions can be physical, emotional, spiritual, or a combination of these.

Constitution (prakriti). Ayurvedic medicine also has specific beliefs about the body's constitution. Constitution refers to a person's general health, the likelihood of becoming out of balance, and the ability to resist and recover from disease or other health problems.

The constitution is called the *prakriti*. The *prakriti* is a person's unique combination of physical and psychological characteristics and the way the body functions to maintain health. It is influenced by such factors as digestion and how the body deals with waste products. The *prakriti* is believed to be unchanged over a person's lifetime.

Life forces (doshas). Important characteristics of the *prakriti* are the three life forces or energies called *doshas*, which control the activities of the body. A person's chances of developing certain types of diseases are thought to be related to the way *doshas* are balanced, the state of the physical body, and mental or lifestyle factors.

Ayurvedic medicine holds the following beliefs about the three *doshas*:

- Each *dosha* is made up of two of five basic elements: ether (the upper regions of space), air, fire, water, and earth.

- Each *dosha* has a particular relationship to bodily functions and can be upset for different reasons.

- Each person has a unique combination of the three *doshas*, although one *dosha* is usually prominent. *Doshas* are constantly being formed and reformed by food, activity, and bodily processes.

- Each *dosha* has its own physical and psychological characteristics.

- An imbalance of a *dosha* will produce symptoms that are unique to that *dosha*. Imbalances may be caused by a person's age, unhealthy lifestyle, or diet; too much or too little mental and physical exertion; the seasons; or inadequate protection from the weather, chemicals, or germs.

The *doshas* are known by their original Sanskrit names: *vata, pitta,* and *kapha.*

The *vata dosha* combines the elements ether and air. It is considered the most powerful *dosha* because it controls very basic body processes such as cell division, the heart, breathing, discharge of waste, and the mind. *Vata* can be aggravated by, for example, fear, grief, staying up late at night, eating dry fruit, or eating before the previous meal is digested. People with *vata* as their main *dosha* are thought to be especially susceptible to skin and neurological conditions, rheumatoid arthritis, heart disease, anxiety, and insomnia.

Ayurvedic treatment is tailored to each person's constitution.

The *pitta dosha* represents the elements fire and water. *Pitta* controls hormones and the digestive system. A person with a *pitta* imbalance may experience negative emotions such as anger and may have physical symptoms such as heartburn within 2 or 3 hours of eating. *Pitta* is upset by, for example, eating spicy or sour food, fatigue, or spending too much time in the sun. People with a predominantly *pitta* constitution are thought to be susceptible to hypertension, heart disease, infectious diseases, and digestive conditions such as Crohn's disease.

The *kapha dosha* combines the elements water and earth. *Kapha* helps to maintain strength and immunity and to control growth. An imbalance of the *kapha dosha* may cause nausea immediately after eating. *Kapha* is aggravated by, for example, greed, sleeping during the daytime, eating too many sweet foods, eating after one is full, and eating and drinking foods and beverages with too much salt and water (especially in the springtime). Those with a predominant *kapha dosha* are thought to be vulnerable to diabetes, cancer, obesity, and respiratory illnesses such as asthma.

Ayurvedic treatment goals include eliminating impurities, reducing symptoms, increasing resistance to disease, and reducing worry and increasing harmony in the patient's life.

Treatment

Ayurvedic treatment is tailored to each person's constitution. Practitioners expect patients to be active participants because many Ayurvedic treatments require changes in diet, lifestyle, and habits.

The patient's dosha balance. Ayurvedic practitioners first determine the patient's primary *dosha* and the balance among the three *doshas* by:

- Asking about diet, behavior, lifestyle practices, recent illnesses (including reasons and symptoms), and resilience (ability to recover quickly from illness or setbacks)

- Observing such physical characteristics as teeth and tongue, skin, eyes, weight, and overall appearance

- Checking the patient's urine, stool, speech and voice, and pulse (each *dosha* is thought to make a particular kind of pulse).

Treatment practices. Ayurvedic treatment goals include eliminating impurities, reducing symptoms, increasing resistance to disease, and reducing worry and increasing harmony in the patient's life. The practitioner uses a variety of methods to achieve these goals:

- *Eliminating impurities.* A process called *panchakarma* is intended to cleanse the body by eliminating *ama*. *Ama* is described as an undigested food that sticks to tissues, interferes with normal functioning of the body, and leads to disease. *Panchakarma* focuses on eliminating *ama* through the digestive tract and the respiratory system. Enemas, massage, medical oils administered in a nasal spray, and other methods may be used.

- *Reducing symptoms.* The practitioner may suggest various options, including physical exercises, stretching, breathing exercises, meditation, massage, lying in the sun, and changing the diet. The patient may take certain herbs—often with honey, to make them easier to digest. Sometimes diets are restricted to certain foods. Very small amounts of metal and mineral preparations, such as gold or iron, also may be given.

- *Increasing resistance to disease.* The practitioner may combine several herbs, proteins, minerals, and vitamins in tonics to improve digestion and increase appetite and immunity. These tonics are based on formulas from ancient texts.

- *Reducing worry and increasing harmony.* Ayurvedic medicine emphasizes mental nurturing and spiritual healing. Practitioners may recommend avoiding situations that cause worry and using techniques that promote release of negative emotions.

Use of plants. Ayurvedic treatments rely heavily on herbs and other plants—including oils and common spices. Currently, more than 600 herbal formulas and 250 single-plant drugs are included in the "pharmacy" of Ayurvedic treatments. Historically, Ayurvedic medicine has grouped plant compounds into categories according to their effects (for example, healing, promoting vitality, or relieving pain). The compounds are described in texts issued by national medical agencies in India. Sometimes, botanicals are mixed with metals or other naturally occurring substances to make formulas prepared according to specific Ayurvedic text procedures; such preparations involve several herbs and herbal extracts and precise heat treatment.

Many practitioners study in India, where there are more than 150 undergraduate and 30 postgraduate colleges for Ayurvedic medicine. Training can take 5 years or longer. Students who receive their Ayurvedic training in India can earn either a bachelor's degree (Bachelor of Ayurvedic Medicine and Surgery, BAMS) or doctoral degree (Doctor of Ayurvedic Medicine and Surgery, DAMS) there. After graduation, some Ayurvedic practitioners choose to provide services in the United States or other countries.

The United States has no national standard for training or certifying Ayurvedic practitioners, although a few states have approved Ayurvedic schools as educational institutions.

Concerns About Ayurvedic Medications

Ayurvedic practice involves the use of medications that typically contain herbs, metals, minerals, or other materials. Health officials in India and other countries have taken steps to address some concerns about these medications. Concerns relate to toxicity, formulations, interactions, and scientific evidence.

Toxicity. Ayurvedic medications have the potential to be toxic. Many materials used in them have not been thoroughly studied in either Western or Indian research. In the United States, Ayurvedic medications are regulated as dietary supplements. As such, they are not required to meet the safety and efficacy standards for conventional medicines. An NCCAM-funded study published in 2004 found that of 70 Ayurvedic remedies purchased over-the-counter (all manufactured in South Asia), 14 contained lead, mercury, and/or arsenic at levels that could be harmful. Also in 2004, the Centers for Disease Control and Prevention reported that 12 cases of lead poisoning occurring over a recent 3-year period were linked to the use of Ayurvedic medications.

Formulations. Most Ayurvedic medications consist of combinations of herbs and other medicines. It can be challenging to know which components are having an effect and why.

Interactions. Whenever two or more medications are used, there is the potential for them to interact with each other. As a result, the effectiveness of at least one may increase or decrease in the body.

Scientific evidence. Most clinical trials (i.e., studies in people) of Ayurvedic approaches have been small, had problems with research designs, lacked appropriate control groups, or had other issues that affected how meaningful the results were. Therefore, scientific evidence for the effectiveness of Ayurvedic practices varies, and more rigorous research is needed to determine which practices are safe and effective.

The Effectiveness and Safety of Ayurvedic Drugs Has Not Been Tested

Meera Nanda

Meera Nanda is an Indian writer, historian, and philosopher of science. She is a fellow at the Jawaharlal Nehru Institute for Advanced Study at the Jawaharlal Nehru University in India, and she is the author of several books.

Charaka, the legendary healer and compiler of *Charaka Samhita*, the ancient textbook of Ayurveda, does not mince words when it comes to the subject of quacks. He calls them "imposters who wear the garb of physicians . . . [who] walk the earth like messengers of death". These fake doctors are "unlearned in scriptures, experience and knowledge of curative operations, but like to boast of their skills before the uneducated". Wise patients, Charaka advises, "should always avoid those foolish men who make a show of learning."

These words, written more than 2,000 years ago, bring to mind those who like to play doctor on Indian television these days. The most famous of all, Swami Ramdev, doles out medical advice to millions of Indians who tune into his show, attend his yoga camps and buy his Ayurvedic drugs. He offers "complete cure", "in weeks, if not in days", of "diseases from A to Z", from "common cold to cancers", including cholera, diabetes, glaucoma, heart disease, kidney disease, leprosy, liver disease . . . so on and so forth. There is practically nothing that his method of Divya yoga, alone, or in combination with his Ayurvedic formulations, cannot cure. And his "miraculous" cures are not merely "confirmed by science", but are, indeed, "science in its purest form". (All quotations are from

Meera Nanda, "Ayurveda Under the Scanner," *Frontline*, vol. 23, April 8, 2006. All rights reserved. Reproduced by permission of the author.

Swami Ramdev's own web site, www.swamiramdev.info). The swami is not alone in making such fantastic claims. Yoga and Ayurveda are being mass-marketed to India's growing middle classes like never before. Putting on a "show of learning" by "wearing the garb" of healers and scientists seems to be good for the guru business.

The recent expose of false labelling of drugs and exploitation of workers at the swami's Haridwar-based pharmacy has created a huge uproar. But *all* the noise and sloganeering is drowning out the real questions that must be asked not just of Ramdev, but of all traditional or alternative medicines: How effective are these medicines in curing the diseases they claim to cure? Can their medical claims pass the muster of rigorously conducted clinical tests? Even if the label on the bottle scrupulously identified each and every "vegetarian" and "non-vegetarian" ingredient, the question still remains if the drugs are effective and safe when measured by the modern standards of scientific research. . . .

Contemporary Ayurvedic medicines routinely—and legally—use 75 ingredients derived from animals.

The Ayurvedic tradition considers *all* substances, whether they come from animals, vegetables, or the earth (that is, minerals) as medicines, provided they are applied in a proper way and for specific purposes. The ancient doctors recommend the use of the following in medical concoctions: bile, fat, marrow, blood, flesh, excreta, urine, skin, semen, bones, tendons, horns, nails, hoofs, hair, bristles and pigments obtained from a variety of animals. This follows as a logical consequence of the Ayurvedic philosophy that like-nourishes-the-like: Flesh is nourished by flesh, blood by blood, fat by fat, bones by cartilage, marrow by marrow, semen by semen, foetus by eggs . . . and so on.

Various classics of Ayurveda recommend a variety of medical treatments that make liberal use of animal products, including cow urine cooked in ghee for treatment of epilepsy, skull bones mixed with cow's urine as a cure for ulcers, and beef, to quote *Charaka Samhita*, for "rhinitis, irregular fever, dry cough, fatigue, heightened digestion, and wasting of muscles". Contemporary Ayurvedic medicines routinely—and legally—use 75 ingredients derived from animals.

Swami Ramdev, then, could be faulted not for using human and animal body parts, but for not disclosing their presence in the drugs he was selling. This lack of transparency is not a trivial matter, for consumers have a right to know what goes into the medicines they depend upon. [Indian politician Brinda] Karat and the workers of Divya Yog [Madir] Trust have undoubtedly brought an important issue to light [when it was found that Ramdev's "herbal medicine" did not contain herbs, but other materials such as human and animal particles].

Is Labelling the Answer?

But proper labelling should be the beginning, not the end, of a serious investigation of the medical claims that are routinely made for Ayurvedic remedies.

Let us imagine that by some miracle, each and every one of the 361,881 licensed Ayurvedic doctors in India begins to abide by the new laws requiring full disclosure and good manufacturing practices. Let us stipulate that all the loopholes have been closed and that all Ayurvedic preparations meant for export or for sale at home, come with detailed information of traditional and botanical names of all the herbs, the names and amounts of all animal and mineral ingredients, the traditional recipes according to which they are made, the batch number, the date of expiry, the risks and contraindications.

Is all this enough to ensure the efficacy and safety of Ayurvedic drugs? Will faithful adherence to traditional recipes produce drugs that work? Unless the ingredients and methods followed by traditional Ayurvedic books *themselves* have been subjected to rigorous clinical and laboratory tests, mere disclosure and good manufacturing practices will not do.

Without an objective understanding of the fundamentals of Ayurveda, and without rigorous, controlled clinical tests of the ancient Ayurvedic formulations, we may end up faithfully reproducing many of their limitations and dangers, along with many of their possible benefits.

The simple truth is that there is a lack of good quality research in Ayurveda.

The simple truth is that there is a lack of good quality research in Ayurveda. Even staunch advocates of Ayurveda like Dr. M.S. Valiathan, an eminent cardiologist, admit that "clinical studies that would satisfy the liberal criteria of WHO [World Health Organization] have been alarmingly few from India, in spite of patients crowding in Ayurvedic hospitals." (India generally follows WHO standards, which do not demand stringent clinical tests for traditional medical systems with long historical traditions.) The general consensus of international experts is that, to quote the National Center for Complementary and Alternative Medicine (NCCAM) in the U.S., "most clinical trials of Ayurvedic approaches have been small, had problems with research designs, lacked appropriate control groups, or had other issues that affected how meaningful the results were."

Science vs. Tradition

This lack of reliable scientific research is partly the result of a deep-seated contradiction between wanting to appear scientific while holding on to ancient traditions. On the one hand, policy makers and the bureaucrats at [the Department of] AY-USH, the government agency responsible for scientific research on Ayurveda, make extravagant promises for "massive research and development" for the purpose of "scientific validation" of Ayurveda. On the other hand, traditional healers and modern gurus continue to insist that no amount of research can alter, or refute, the "Eternal and Absolute Truths" of Ayurveda, which were supposedly revealed to the Vedic seers at the very "beginning of time". Even AYUSH describes Ayurveda as having "originated with the origin of the universe itself". (What could this possibly mean?)

This anxiety to affirm our ancient traditions has led to a deep and widespread confirmation bias in research on traditional sciences. Ayurvedic researchers, in other words, tend to look for and notice only what confirms their existing beliefs, while they either do not look for, or ignore and explain away, the evidence that contradicts their beliefs. Indian intellectuals and scientists, moreover, have been only too ready to find fanciful analogies between advances in modern biology and the traditional concepts of body and disease.

Years of this kind of advocacy research has created a big problem. The problem is that traditional medical formulae and recipes have not been put to a systematic test using the best available scientific knowledge, methodology and instrumentation available today. Their claims for curing diseases are entirely based on traditional lore, anecdotal evidence and the authority of gurus.

As a result, many obsolete and even harmful chemicals, methods of diagnosis and procedures still continue to be prescribed. What is worse, many of them are presented to the public *as if* they have been validated by advances in modern science and medicine. As Dr. R.A. Mashelkar, the Director of the Council for Scientific and Industrial Research (CSIR), recommended in his famous "Golden Triangle" speech (where he spoke of building a golden triangle between traditional medicine, modern medicine and modern science), there is a need to "trim" Ayurvedic products so that we can rationally understand what works and what does not, what is healthful and what is harmful, what is living and what is dead in traditional Indian medicine. . . .

Many obsolete and even harmful chemicals, methods of diagnosis and procedures still continue to be prescribed.

Toxic Heavy Metals

A 2004 study published in the *Journal of the American Medical Association (JAMA)* found significant levels of toxic heavy metals such as mercury, lead, and arsenic in 20 per cent of Ayurvedic preparations that were made in India and went for sale in America. The situation is far worse in India where 64 per cent of samples collected were found to contain significant amounts of mercury, arsenic and cadmium.

In the wake of the bad publicity created by the *JAMA* report, the Indian government wants all export-quality drugs to certify that their heavy-metal content is within the acceptable limits. Ironically, drugs intended for domestic consumption are to remain free from such requirements, at least until the time more laboratories for testing this are established.

It is in the attempt to explain and control the toxic levels of heavy metals that the lack of rigorous science shows up. Some of the contamination could no doubt be due to environmental pollution and "unsatisfactory agricultural and cultivation practices", as AYUSH has tried to explain. But at the same time, by agreeing to initiate chemical analysis and animal studies for toxicity of eight *bhasams*, AYUSH has tacitly admitted that the problem could be integral to these medicines themselves. According to Dr. P. Viswanathan, all eight formulations contain heavy metals well-known for their toxicity: Kajjali is a powder of mercury and sulphur, Rasmanikya is tri-sulphide of arsenic, Nag Bhasama is a *bhasam* of lead, Rasasindoor is a *bhasam* containing mercury and sulphur. The other four drugs—Basantkusumkar Ras, Arogyavardhini Vati, Mahayograj Guggul and Mahalaxmi Vilas Ras—contain mixtures of all common *bhasams*, and are extensively used for diabetes, liver disease, arthritis and respiratory diseases.

The presence of toxic heavy metals in Ayurvedic preparations is not surprising. . . .

There is . . . a long and well-respected tradition of using heavy metals in Ayurveda. But, after so many years of promising us a scientific account of Ayurveda, we know practically nothing about what happens to these metals when they are subjected to the traditional processes of *sodhana* and *bhasmikaran*. We constantly hear assurances from the proponents of Ayurveda that the traditional process of turning heavy metals into *bhasams* "detoxifies" them and makes them harmless. The message is that if the manufacturers faithfully followed the instructions in the classic Ayurvedic texts, there would be no problem of toxicity.

Anecdotal evidence of people reporting that they are feeling better cannot provide sufficient grounds for "scientific" validation of Ayurveda or any other kind of medicine.

But we are supposed to accept these assurances of faith alone, for they are not based upon any actual research. We do not even know, after all these years of "research", if the process of making *bhasams* turns these heavy metals into oxides or some other kind of compound altogether. According to Dr. C. Viswanathan, an orthopaedic surgeon who is also well versed in Ayurveda, "the oxide of mercury is certainly toxic and is a health problem. . . . I think it is just wishful thinking to suggest that any amount of baking with herbs is going to make mercury non-poisonous." . . .

Lack of Evidence

As a final case, let us look at Swami Ramdev's prescription of *parnayam* as a "miraculous" cure for "all diseases, from A to Z". Ramdev lists some 260 conditions, including infectious diseases (cholera, leprosy, syphilis), hormonal disorders (diabetes, thyroid disorders) and complex, life-threatening, systemic diseases of heart, liver, kidneys, brain, reproductive system. Yoga and *parnayam* (deep breathing exercises) alone, he promises, can "completely" cure all of these ailments. He claims that patients show significant improvements in their blood-sugar level, blood pressure, cholesterol and triglyceride levels, lung functioning and obesity by doing yoga and *parnayam* for just eight days in the "yoga-science" camps he organised periodically through 2004–05.

There are undeniable benefits of yoga. But curing diabetes? Curing infectious diseases? There is no credible scientific evidence for any of these claims. In the refereed medical literature, yoga has only shown some benefit for reducing hypertension (that too, only in combination with aerobic exercises and extremely low-fat diets). There are also some reports that show marginal and short-lived improvement for asthma and carpal tunnel syndrome (a condition affecting the hand and wrist). Yoga is also shown to improve strength and flexibility, but not any more than other physical exercises, including walking.

Can Ramdev's claims for "miraculous cures" be trusted? His "scientific evidence" does not meet even the most minimum standards of clinical trials. But the poor quality of evidence seems to be almost beside the point in the debates about Ayurveda. The majority of those who believe in Swami Ramdev's cures seem to be convinced by anecdotes and personal stories they hear from friends, relatives, and from those who testify on television. . . .

Anecdotal evidence of people reporting that they are feeling better cannot provide sufficient grounds for "scientific" validation of Ayurveda or any other kind of medicine.

We have heard many claims of Ayurveda and yoga being the "complete" and "highest" sciences. It is time now to expose these ancient sciences to the test of medical and biological sciences, as we understand them today.

Toward that end, it will be useful to keep in mind the wise words of Marcia Angell and Jerome Kassirer from their famous 1998 editorial in the *New England Journal of Medicine*:

> "There cannot be two kinds of medicines—conventional and alternative. *There is only medicine that has been adequately tested and medicine that has not, medicine that works and medicine that may or may not work.* . . . Alternative treatments should be subjected to scientific testing no less rigorous than that required for conventional treatments."

Charaka would have certainly agreed. After all, it was Charaka who advised his fellow healers to "always strive to acquire knowledge. There is no end of medical science. Hence, heedfully thou shouldst devote thyself to it. . . . And even if possessed of sufficient knowledge, thou shouldst not boast of that knowledge."

Naturopathy Aims Not Only to Treat Disease but Also to Restore Health

American Association of Naturopathic Physicians

The American Association of Naturopathic Physicians is the national, professional society representing licensed or licensable naturopathic physicians who completed a four-year, residential graduate program.

Naturopathic medicine is based on the belief that the human body has an innate healing ability. Naturopathic doctors (NDs) teach their patients to use diet, exercise, lifestyle changes and cutting-edge natural therapies to enhance their bodies' ability to ward off and combat disease. NDs view the patient as a complex, interrelated system (a whole person), not as a clogged artery or a tumor. Naturopathic physicians craft comprehensive treatment plans that blend the best of modern medical science and traditional natural medical approaches to not only treat disease, but to also restore health.

Naturopathic physicians base their practice on six timeless principles founded on medical tradition and scientific evidence.

- *Let nature heal.* Our bodies have such a powerful, innate instinct for self-healing. By finding and removing the barriers to this self-healing—such as poor diet or unhealthy habits—naturopathic physicians can nurture this process.

- *Identify and treat causes.* Naturopathic physicians understand that symptoms will only return unless the root illness is addressed. Rather than cover up symptoms, they seek to find and treat the cause of these symptoms.

* *First, do no harm.* Naturopathic physicians follow three precepts to ensure their patients' safety:

    Use low-risk procedures and healing compounds—such as dietary supplements, herbal extracts and homeopathy—with few or no side effects.

    When possible, do not suppress symptoms, which are the body's efforts to self-heal. For example, the body may cook up a fever in reaction to a bacterial infection. Fever creates an inhospitable environment for the harmful bacteria, thereby destroying it. Of course, the naturopathic physician would not allow the fever to get dangerously high.

    Customize each diagnosis and treatment plan to fit each patient. We all heal in different ways and the naturopathic physician respects our differences.

* *Educate patients.* Naturopathic medicine believes that doctors must be educators, as well as physicians. That's why naturopathic physicians teach their patients how to eat, exercise, relax and nurture themselves physically and emotionally. They also encourage self-responsibility and work closely with each patient.

* *Treat the whole person.* We each have a unique physical, mental, emotional, genetic, environmental, social, sexual and spiritual makeup. The naturopathic physician knows that all these factors affect our health. That's why he or she includes them in a carefully tailored treatment strategy.

* *Prevent illness.* "An ounce of prevention is worth a pound of cure" has never been truer. Proactive medi-

cine saves money, pain, misery and lives. That's why naturopathic physicians evaluate risk factors, heredity and vulnerability to disease. By getting treatment for greater wellness, we're less likely to need treatment for future illness.

By using protocols that minimize the risk of harm, naturopathic physicians help facilitate the body's inherent ability to restore and maintain optimal health.

What Is a Naturopathic Doctor?

Naturopathic physicians combine the wisdom of nature with the rigors of modern science. Steeped in traditional healing methods, principles and practices, naturopathic medicine focuses on holistic, proactive prevention and comprehensive diagnosis and treatment. By using protocols that minimize the risk of harm, naturopathic physicians help facilitate the body's inherent ability to restore and maintain optimal health. It is the naturopathic physician's role to identify and remove barriers to good health by helping to create a healing internal and external environment.

Naturopathic physicians work in private practices, hospitals, clinics and community health centers. NDs practice throughout the United States and Canada. Qualified naturopathic physicians undergo rigorous training before they become licensed healthcare practitioners. . . .

NDs treat all medical conditions and can provide both individual and family healthcare. Among the most common ailments they treat are allergies, chronic pain, digestive issues, hormonal imbalances, obesity, respiratory conditions, heart disease, fertility problems, menopause, adrenal fatigue, cancer, fibromyalgia and chronic fatigue syndrome. NDs can perform minor surgeries, such as removing cysts or stitching up superficial wounds. However, they do not practice major surgery.

NDs are trained to utilize prescription drugs, although the emphasis of naturopathic medicine is the use of natural healing agents.

A naturopathic physician will take time with you. During your first appointment, your doctor will take your health history, find out about your diet, stress levels, use of tobacco and alcohol, and discuss why you're there. He or she may perform an examination and order diagnostic tests. Naturopathic physicians keep themselves up to date on the latest scientific research and incorporate this evidence into their treatments. The naturopathic physician will work with you to set up a customized health management strategy. If necessary, your doctor will refer you to other healthcare practitioners.

A first visit with a patient may last one to two hours and follow-up visits range from 30 to 60 minutes, although this varies depending on the ND. Naturopathic physicians need sufficient time to ask questions and understand the patient's health goals. NDs also need time to gather information, do an appropriate examination and teach his or her patients about managing their condition and improving their health. An ND may also use diagnostic tests to fully understand their patient's health status. Besides taking the time to carefully and fully assess a patient's root problem, NDs speak and understand the language of conventional medicine. They can diagnose the way MDs [doctors of medicine] do—yet, they bring to the patient a whole new arsenal of treatments and insights. Instead of waiting for a disease to emerge, NDs work to head it off before it happens.

There Is No Evidence to Support the Claims of Naturopathy

Robert T. Carroll

Robert T. Carroll is a retired teacher of philosophy who wrote The Skeptic's Dictionary: A Collection of Strange Beliefs, Amusing Deceptions and Dangerous Delusions *and other books; he now operates the Skeptic's Dictionary website.*

Naturopathy is a system of therapy and treatment which relies exclusively on natural remedies, such as sunlight, air, water, supplemented with diet and therapies such as massage. However, some naturopaths have been known to prescribe such unnatural treatments as colon hydrotherapy for such diseases as asthma and arthritis.

Naturopathy is based on the belief that the body is self-healing. The body will repair itself and recover from illness spontaneously if it is in a healthy environment. Naturopaths have many remedies and recommendations for creating a healthy environment so the body can spontaneously heal itself.

Naturopaths claim to be holistic, which means they believe that the natural body is joined to a supernatural soul and a nonphysical mind and the three must be treated as a unit, whatever that means. Naturopathy is fond of such terms as "balance" and "harmony" and "energy." It is often rooted in mysticism and a metaphysical belief in vitalism.

Unsubstantiated Claims

Naturopaths are also prone to make grandiose claims about some herb or remedy that can enhance the immune system. Yet, only medical doctors are competent to do the tests necessary to determine if an individual's immune system is in any way depressed. Naturopaths assume that many diseases, including cancer, are caused by faulty immune systems. (The immune system, in simple terms, is the body's own set of mechanisms that attacks anything that isn't "self." Although, in some cases rather than attack "foreign bodies" such as viruses, fungi, or bacteria, the immune response goes haywire and the body attacks its own cells, e.g., in lupus, multiple sclerosis, and rheumatoid arthritis.) Naturopaths also promote the idea that the *mind* can be used to enhance the immune system and thereby improve one's health. However Dr. Saul Green argues that

> there are no reports in the scientific literature to support the contention that any AM [alternative medicine] operates through an established immunological mechanism. Regardless of the means used to evoke an antitumor response, all the evidence available from clinical and animal studies clearly shows that only after the attention of the NIS [normal immune system] has been attracted by some external manipulation of its components, is there any recognition by NIS of the existence of the tumor. All the evidence amassed over the past 30 years provides a clear answer to the question, "Does any AM treatment stimulate the NIS and cause it to identify and destroy new cancer cells when they appear?" The answer clearly is NO!

There is no scientific evidence that any of these [naturopathic] remedies either enhance the immune system or make it possible for the body to heal itself.

Furthermore, the evidence that such diseases as cancer occur mainly in people with compromised immune systems is lacking. This is an assumption made by many naturopaths but it is not supported by the scientific evidence. Immunologists have shown that the most common cancers flourish in hosts with fully functional and competent immune systems. The notion that vitamins and colloidal minerals, herbs, coffee enemas, colonic irrigation, Laetrile [amygdalin, a potentially toxic substance], meditation, etc., can enhance the immune system and thereby help restore health is bogus. On the one hand, it is not necessarily the case that a diseased person even has a compromised immune system. On the other hand, there is no scientific evidence that any of these remedies either enhance the immune system or make it possible for the body to heal itself.

Naturopathy is often, if not always, practiced in combination with other forms of "alternative" health practices. Bastyr University, a leading school of naturopathy since 1978, offers instruction in such things as acupuncture and "spirituality." Much of the advice of naturopaths is sound: exercise, quit smoking, eat lots of fresh fruits and vegetables, practice good nutrition. Claims that these and practices such as colonic irrigation or coffee enemas "detoxify" the body or enhance the immune system or promote "homeostasis," "harmony," "balance," "vitality," and the like are exaggerated and not backed up by sound research.

Should the Government Restrict the Use of Alternative Therapies?

Chapter Preface

The most contentious issue with regard to complementary and alternative therapies is the question of to what extent, if any, they should be regulated by the government. On one hand, many science-oriented people feel strongly that any therapy for which there is no scientific evidence should be discouraged and perhaps banned. On the other hand, advocates of individual freedom believe that for the government to interfere in personal health care decisions is no less a violation of liberty than interference with free speech or freedom of religion.

This conflict arises from a fundamental difference in philosophy that underlies American society. Some people believe that it is the responsibility of the government to protect everyone from possible harm that may result from their own decisions. Others believe that the only legitimate function of government is to protect people from harm intentionally inflicted by others, such as criminals or foreign aggressors. In a democracy, any decision about the role of government in medical care must be a compromise between these two positions.

It is often argued that there is a long-standing mandate for the government to protect public health. This is true, but in earlier times "public health" meant only the control of contagious disease and other situations where one person's actions would be likely to cause sickness of others. The Supreme Court's 1901 decision supporting compulsory vaccination that is frequently cited as the basis of government health regulations was intended to prevent the spread of contagious disease. At that time no one thought of applying it to things that would harm only the people who chose them; even narcotics were legally sold over the counter until 1914. Prescription drugs did not require a doctor's authorization until 1938, and some people still believe they should not be regulated except to the extent of requiring accurate labeling.

The involvement of government in medical care has mushroomed during the last half century, and with the health care reform act of 2010, which as of 2011 is being challenged as unconstitutional, it has grown still more. In part, this was because the government now pays for much of American medical research and for treatment through insurance programs such as Medicare. Another factor was the increasing power of bureaucracies whose scope now extends far beyond what was originally established. Still another was that many people felt a need for authoritative evaluation of the ever-more-complex medical technologies of the late twentieth century.

Resisting this trend are the health freedom movement, a loosely organized group fighting to preserve the unregulated status of nutritional supplements; the anti-vaccination movement, composed of people who believe that some vaccines are harmful and that in any case the government has no right to dictate what is put into their children's bodies; users of alternate therapies who consider much in conventional medicine to be wrong; and libertarians who hold, as a matter of principle, that above all government should respect individual freedom. Opposed to them are people who are convinced that public policy should be based on scientific evidence, and that even though such evidence is statistical rather than a determination of what is best for any given individual, reason demands that adherence to it be given more weight than respect for personal opinions.

The science advocates are absolutely sure that science and science alone reveals truth, while many of their antagonists maintain that experience also counts and that scientific theories change from era to era. They point out that in the nineteenth century homeopathy and allopathy (the form of medicine now considered conventional) competed for dominance and that allopathy's victory was at least partially due to the

American Medical Association's political success in gaining a monopoly on the licensing of physicians. Complicating this debate is the fact that science is beginning to discover that some therapies previously thought to be biologically impossible may be more effective than limited knowledge suggested—for example, in 2010 researchers using brain scanning found that the activation of brain areas involved in pain perception is significantly reduced during acupuncture.

Emotions run high on both sides of this controversy and are often expressed with little tolerance for disagreement. It is not just a matter of who is right about the value of alternative medicine. Even supposing that there is irrefutable proof that conventional medicine is always superior, say freedom defenders, human beings have an inalienable right to be wrong and to take the consequences of their own choices concerning medical care.

Protecting Public Health Is the Responsibility of the Government

Brennen McKenzie

Brennen McKenzie is a practicing veterinarian.

When I write or talk about the scientific evidence against particular alternative medical approaches, I am frequently asked the question, "So, if it doesn't work, why is it legal?" Believers in CAM [complementary and alternative medicine] ask this to show that there must be something to what they are promoting or, presumably, the government wouldn't let them sell it. And skeptics raise the question often out of sheer incredulity that anyone would be allowed to make money selling a medical therapy that doesn't work. It turns out that the answer to this question is a complex, multilayered story involving science, history, politics, religion, and culture.

While we science types tend to be primarily interested in what is true and what isn't, that is a sometimes surprisingly minor factor in the process of constructing laws and regulations concerning medicine. . . .

Freedom vs. Protection

There is a deep ideological divide in America on the subject of who is responsible for ensuring that the products we buy are safe and perform as advertised, and the area of medicine is not exempt from this political debate. On one extreme is the self-identified "health freedom" lobby, which argues that the consumer and the market should be the only forces to regulate healthcare products and services. As an example, economist Randall Holcombe has written:

An auto mechanic does not have to be a medical expert to use market information to find good health care, any more than a doctor has to be an automobile expert to find a good car. . . . Deregulation not only provides incentives for patients to look for, and physicians to offer, better care, it permits all parties concerned the freedom to decide what better care is. For instance, in the debate over alternative medicine, such as herbal treatments, chiropractors, acupuncture, and so on, the question is not only whether alternative medicine is effective, but whether people should be allowed to use these alternatives even if their physical health may not improve or may even suffer. . . . In a free country, people should be free to choose whatever health care options they want for whatever purpose . . . even if health care professionals believe that care is substandard.

There is a deep ideological divide in America on the subject of who is responsible for ensuring that the products we buy are safe and perform as advertised.

Those more sympathetic to laws and regulations intended to protect consumers from unsafe and ineffective therapies argue against this concept of "medical anarchism" [as quoted in D.W. Ramey and B.E. Rollin, "Untested Therapies and Medical Anarchism"]:

Why not let the market decide? Why not trust the citizenry to sort out what works from what doesn't work in medicine as we do in other aspects of life?

The answer has to do with knowledge and risk. People do let the market decide with regard to goods like ice cream cones and baseball bats, and services like travel booking. If the ice cream is not good, people won't buy it; if the service is defective, people will go elsewhere. However, in such situations, people are easily able to evaluate the quality and value of the goods and services they receive. . . . Nor are such services administered under duress, nor are they represented as necessary for one's health or well-being. . . .

But in the area of medicine, too much is at stake. If one chooses the wrong therapeutic modality, once can lose health, life, and limb. Furthermore, few individuals are sufficiently wealthy, educated, or possessed of the resources to test putative medical therapies. In fact, there are so many putative therapies, that it is impossible for an individual to try them all. When people are ill, they do not have time to test even a handful.

The self-evident notion that it is the role of government to protect the public from quackery turns out not to be self-evident to many Americans.

These arguments tend to run in parallel, and to be only tenuously connected, with the usual focus of this blog; the question of how one evaluates medical therapies and what the evaluation indicates about safety and efficacy. Of course, many proponents of CAM who invoke the "health freedom" position do actually believe the therapies they promote are beneficial. But the fundamental position itself does not hinge on this, since from a perspective such as Dr. Holcombe's people should be free to choose even therapies that are ineffective or harmful without "burdensome" government regulatory interference. The self-evident notion that it is the role of government to protect the public from quackery turns out not to be self-evident to many Americans, and thus demonstrating that a given approach is quackery may not be sufficient to convince them that it should be prohibited or even officially discouraged.

The Right to Privacy vs. State Police Powers

In the legal arena, the political conflict between those favoring or opposing aggressive consumer protection regulations in the area of healthcare takes the form of statutes and judicial opinions balancing the competing constitutional principles of an individual right to privacy and a governmental authority, or even mandate, to protect the public health. Neither a right to privacy or absolute authority over one's own body nor a government role in regulating healthcare are specifically mentioned in the U.S. Constitution, but both are held to exist by long-standing interpretation. A right to privacy, including control over one's own body and the care of it, is generally believed to be established by a broad reading of the 14th Amendment, though there is some controversy about this as about most areas of constitutional law. The authority of the state to abrogate this right in the process of protecting the public health is usually understood to be based in the "police powers" established by the 10th Amendment.

In 1824, the Supreme Court made reference to "health laws of every description" as encompassed within the "state police powers," those powers not specifically delegated to the federal government nor prohibited to the states which are thus held, under the 10th Amendment, to be the prerogative of the individual states. The court cited and expanded this opinion in a subsequent case in 1905, in which a state mandate to protect the public health was held to override, at least in some circumstances, the individual right to control one's own body. The case involved a man prosecuted for refusing a mandatory smallpox vaccination. The opinion stated:

> The authority of the state to enact this statute is to be referred to what is commonly called the police power ... this court ... distinctly recognized the authority of a state to enact quarantine laws and "health laws of every description...."

> The defendant insists that his liberty is invaded when the state subjects him to fine or imprisonment for neglecting or refusing to submit to vaccination ... and that the execution of such a law ... is nothing short of an assault upon his person. But the liberty secured by the Constitution of the

United States . . . does not import an absolute right in each person to be, at all times and in all circumstances, wholly freed from restraint. There are manifold restraints to which every person is necessarily subject for the common good.

[The Supreme Court] concluded that under at least some circumstances the authority to protect the public health trumps the right of an individual to control his or her own body.

The court went on to specifically balance the "liberty secured by the 14th Amendment," including "the control of one's body" against "the power of the public to guard itself against imminent danger" and concluded that under at least some circumstances the authority to protect the public health trumps the right of an individual to control his or her own body.

This precedent was further developed and expanded in subsequent cases to validate the state's authority to define and regulate medical practices, to control what practices could be offered and by whom via licensing and scope-of-practice laws, and to prohibit individuals from choosing specific medical treatments if these were considered to be ineffective or dangerous. . . . The legal basis for the regulations of medical practice which today pertain to CAM, as well as scientific medicine, is generally seen by the courts as a balance between the individual right to privacy and the state authority to protect public health.

Philosophy and Politics vs. Scientific Fact

I feel it is important to emphasize again that the question of the medical facts in such cases, and how these are established, are not always seen by the courts to be as relevant as the legal or political issues. For example, in *Jacobson v. Massachusetts* the court specifically addressed the factual claims by the defendant that the vaccine was ineffective and unsafe. The court's reasoning will seem familiar, and disturbing, to those of us dealing with the anti-vaccination movement today:

> The appellant claims that vaccination does not tend to prevent smallpox, but tends to bring about other diseases, and that it does much harm, with no good. It must be conceded that some laymen, both learned and unlearned, and some physicians of great skill and repute, do not believe that vaccination is a preventative of smallpox. The common belief, however, is that it has a decided tendency to prevent the spread of this fearful disease. . . . While not accepted by all, it is accepted by the mass of the people, as well as by most members of the medical profession. . . . A common belief, like common knowledge, does not require evidence to establish its existence, but may be acted upon without proof by the legislature and the courts. . . . The fact that the belief may be wrong, and that science may yet show it to be wrong, is not conclusive; for the legislature has the right to pass laws which, according to the common belief of the people, are adapted to prevent the spread of contagious diseases. In a free country, where the government is by the people, through their chosen representatives, practical legislation admits of no other standard of action, for what the people believe is for the common welfare must be accepted as tending to promote the common welfare, whether it does in fact or not. Any other basis would conflict with the spirit of the Constitution, and would sanction measures opposed to a Republican form of government.

While the decision in this case, to support the authority of the state to enforce mandatory vaccination as a public health measure, might be welcomed by supporters of science-based public health policy, the decision itself was by no means based in science or scientific reasoning.

The laws and judicial opinions which govern the practice of medicine may sometimes support and sometimes oppose legitimate, science and evidence-based medicine. But the legislators, lawyers, and judges responsible for these laws and opinions are not scientists, and their reasoning about scientific and medical issues often has a philosophical and epistemological basis often incompatible with the scientific approach. Such policy mistakes as DSHEA [Dietary Supplement Health and Education Act] and NCCAM [National Center for Complementary and Alternative Medicine] are much easier to understand, and hopefully prevent, if we clearly understand this.

We must be aware of the limitations of scientific and fact-based arguments in persuading legislators and judges, as well as the general public.

If we are to be effective at promoting scientific medicine and containing unscientific approaches and ineffective or unsafe therapies, we must be aware of the limitations of scientific and fact-based arguments in persuading legislators and judges, as well as the general public. Though science and facts derived from scientific knowledge and investigation must be the foundation of our medical approach, they are not always the most effective means of making the case for this approach, even with our colleagues much less with the citizens, politicians, and legal professionals who ultimately control what sort of influence and oversight government has on medicine. Nonscientists tend to view debates about regulation of CAM in terms of individual rights, consumer protection, truth-in-advertising, fair competition in the marketplace, and other such political and philosophical frames which are as important, or even more important, to them as the issue of what is factually true about CAM and whether particular therapies help or harm. . . .

The kinds of questions that arise in this process may initially seem odd to those of us accustomed to a straightforward emphasis on the relevant facts and evidence. Are doctors allowed to offer unproven or even clearly bogus therapies? Are they *required* to offer them if a patient wants them? Can a mainstream doctor be sued for providing or failing to provide an alternative therapy? Can an alternative practitioner be sued for providing, or failing to provide, mainstream scientific medical care? Can and should patients have whatever care they want regardless of whether science supports it? And from my perspective as a veterinarian, since pets are legally property not persons, is there *any* legal or regulatory control over alternative veterinary medicine at all? Such questions and the reasoning behind asking and answering them, shapes the landscape within which we operate as healthcare providers and advocates for science-based medicine.

The Government Should Force Minors to Accept Conventional Medical Treatment

Steven Novella

Steven Novella is a clinical neurologist at Yale School of Medicine. He is the president of the New England Skeptical Society, and the host and producer of the weekly science podcast, The Skeptics' Guide to the Universe.

Daniel Hauser is a 13-year-old boy suffering from a form of blood cancer called Hodgkin's lymphoma. His oncologist is recommending a standard course of chemotherapy. I do not know the clinical details of this case, but overall, with current treatments, the 5-year survival for childhood Hodgkin's lymphoma is 78%. Without treatment, Daniel's chance of survival drops to 5%.

Despite this Daniel is refusing chemotherapy, and his family is supporting his decision. If Daniel were an adult that would be the end of the story—competent adults have the right to refuse any intervention for whatever reason they choose. But Daniel is a minor, so the state has a duty to protect him, even from his own parents and himself.

Daniel's family are members of the Nemenhah religion, a Native American religious tradition that preaches that the journey from sick to healthy is a spiritual journey. They only use "natural" remedies and refuse modern medical intervention. Dan Zwakman, a member of the Nemenhah religious group, is arguing that this is a case of religious freedom, saying that "our religion is our medicine."

While the beliefs of the Nemenhah religion are in the style of Native American beliefs, the bottom line is the same as Christian Scientists or any other religion that preaches that sickness and health are a spiritual matter that should be treated spiritually, and reliance on modern medicine demonstrates a lack of faith.

Parents are not generally allowed to refuse standard medical care for their children, regardless of the reason. This is considered criminal neglect.

The issues here are therefore well-trodden territory. Our society respects the religious freedom of adults, even if their faith leads them to refuse lifesaving medical interventions. But parents are not generally allowed to refuse standard medical care for their children, regardless of the reason. This is considered criminal neglect. In some states in the US, however, believers have managed to get laws passed which shield them from prosecution for neglect if they refuse standard medical care on behalf of their children.

My position on this is probably similar to the majority opinion—children are not yet mature enough to make life and death decisions for themselves, and parents do not have the right to condemn their own children to death or morbidity in order to serve their own religious beliefs. The state has a right and a duty to protect and care for children until they become adults. I reject the arguments of those who claim that their freedom to practice their religion trumps the responsibility to provide basic care for children.

But this is a debate that will likely be fought over and over again.

CAM as Religion

While investigating this case I also found it interesting that there is a significant overlap between many of the claims of the Nemenhah religion and new age alternative medicine claims. Both groups (CAM [complementary and alternative medicine] advocates and advocates of religions whose faiths conflict with modern medicine) preach "health care freedom." Of course in this context "health care freedom" serves the exact same role as "academic freedom" to creationists—as an argument to subvert reasonable and necessary standards.

It also seems that while there are those who are sincere in their Nemenhah beliefs, others have exploited the religion simply to sell supplements or practice medicine under the cover of religion, using the "Native American" angle as a selling point. "Payments" are explicitly referred to as "donations" or "offerings" with disclaimers that the exchange of money for healing is not a commercial transaction.

The lines between religion and so-called "alternative medicine" are indeed very blurred, and increasingly so. What concerns me the most is that religious freedom is being used as a get-out-of-jail-free card to avoid regulations designed to protect consumers from fraud or incompetence. Anyone now can practice medicine and sell medical products and services if they are couched in religious or even just spiritual jargon.

Regulatory agencies are caught in a bind—they are easily sapped of their confidence and enthusiasm for pursuing a case when the religion card is played. I have personally seen this myself—once regulators get a whiff of religious issues in a case they immediately back off and become reluctant to get involved. Some CAM proponents have therefore exploited this as a mechanism to shield themselves from scrutiny and regulation.

This is a conversation the public needs to have, and regulations need to catch up with reality. A reasonable balance between religious freedom and preventing exploitation and fraud needs to be accommodated.

In my opinion the case of Daniel is similar to the recent case of the 9-month-old Australian girl, Gloria Thomas, who died from untreated eczema—a severe skin condition that left her skin thin and cracked allowing her to become infected. Her father, Thomas Sam, decided to treat her exclusively with homeopathy and consulted other homeopaths and naturopaths for treatment. His faith in homeopathy lead him to watch his young daughter slowly die rather than seek conventional care.

Children likely do not have a sufficient understanding of life-and-death medical decisions to shoulder the burden of such decisions themselves.

Decision on Daniel

There is good news for Daniel Hauser, however. Recently a judge determined that his parents were guilty of medical neglect. While Daniel will not be removed from their custody, they have until May 19 [2009] to find him an oncologist and go through with standard treatment for his cancer.

The judge ruled: "(Daniel has a) rudimentary understanding at best of the risks and benefits of chemotherapy. . . . He does not believe he is ill currently. The fact is that he is very ill currently."

This affirms what I was saying above—children likely do not have a sufficient understanding of life-and-death medical decisions to shoulder the burden of such decisions themselves. In similar cases judges will typically make an individual decision for teenagers, rather than ruling solely based upon their age. In this case, it seems, Daniel does not understand or acknowledge his medical condition.

Daniel's court-appointed attorney, Philip Elbert, is quoted as saying: "I feel it's a blow to families. It marginalizes the decisions that parents face every day in regard to their children's medical care. It really affirms the role that big government is better at making our decisions for us."

I know lawyers are advocates, but this is complete nonsense—the ruling does no such thing. Elbert is treating this decision in this specific case as if it is legislation making all children wards of the state for medical decisions. Rather, this and other cases amount to only the most extreme cases of medical neglect forcing the state to reluctantly step in to protect the health of the child.

Daniel's mother, Colleen Hauser, is also quoted as saying: "My son is not in any medical danger at this point." Given that Daniel has a potentially fatal cancer that was reduced after initial chemotherapy, but then has grown after Daniel refused further treatment, this statement is delusional. That, in my opinion, warrants the state stepping in.

In practice parents are given significant leeway in making medical decisions for their children and only the most extreme cases are brought before the courts, and even then the parents are given primary consideration.

Apparently Daniel himself is a medicine man and elder in the Nemenhah band, the primary belief of which is to treat illness with natural remedies. This is an almost complete mixture of religion and new age alternative medicine philosophies. This is no different than treating severe eczema with homeopathy, except the "philosophy-based" medical beliefs are cloaked in religion.

I hope that Daniel lives long enough to reevaluate his decision from a more mature perspective.

[Editor's note: Daniel and his mother fled the state to escape treatment, but after a warrant was issued for her arrest, they returned voluntarily. Daniel completed the treatments, which were called successful.]

Parents of Children Who Die from Reliance on Alternative Therapies Should Go to Prison

Phil Plait

Phil Plait is an astronomer, lecturer, and writer. He is the author of two books and operates the award-winning blog Bad Astronomy.

Homeopathy is the antiscientific belief that infinitely diluted medicine in water can cure various ailments. It's perhaps the most ridiculous of all "alternative" medicines, since it *clearly* cannot work, *does* not work, and has been tested repeatedly and shown to be useless.

And for those who ask, "what's the harm?", you may direct your question to Thomas Sam and his wife Manju Sam, whose nine-month-old daughter died because of their homeopathic beliefs.

The infant girl, Gloria Thomas, died of complications due to eczema. *Eczema*. This is an easily treatable skin condition (the treatments don't cure eczema but do manage it), but that treatment was withheld from the baby girl by her parents, who rejected the advice of doctors and instead used homeopathic treatments. The baby's condition got worse, with her skin covered in rashes and open cracks. These cracks let in germs which her tiny body had difficulty fighting off. She became undernourished as she used all her nutrients to fight infections instead of for growth and the other normal body functions of an infant. She was constantly sick and in pain, but her parents stuck with homeopathy. When the baby girl

Phil Plait, "Homeopathy Kills," *Bad Astronomy*, June 5, 2009, www.blogs.discover magazine.com/badastronomy.

developed an eye infection, her parents finally took her to a hospital, but it was far too late: little Gloria Thomas succumbed to septicemia from the infection.

Their belief in a clearly wrong antiscientific medical practice killed their baby.

Thomas and Manju Sam were convicted yesterday [June 4, 2009] of manslaughter in Australian court. As a parent myself I cannot even begin to imagine the pain they are going through, the anguish and the emotional horror. But let us be clear here: Their belief in a clearly wrong antiscientific medical practice killed their baby. Homeopathy doesn't work, but because they were raised in an environment that supports belief in homeopathy, they trusted it. They used it, and they rejected real, science-based medicine. And their daughter suffered the consequences.

And suffer she did. The accounts of the pediatricians who tried too late to help little Gloria Thomas are simply harrowing.

Every time I hear about something like this—a baby dying due to "alternative" medicine, or the lies and disinformation from the anti-vaccination movement, or some other belief system that flies in the face of reality—a little bit of me dies as well. I held my daughter shortly after she was born, and I would have done anything to protect her, and that included and still includes protecting her against people who fight so adamantly against reality.

The reality is that the anti-vaxxers' work will result in babies dying. The reality is that belief in homeopathy will result in more babies dying. The reality is that denying science-based medicine will result in more babies dying.

And I know these words will fall on many deaf ears. And I will guarantee the comments to this post will contain many loud and irrational arguments supporting homeopathy and the anti-vaxxers. I've seen it before, and I know that many of those people are completely immune to reason and logic. And if you wonder what might wake them up, the answer may very well be nothing. Just read what Gloria Thomas's father—the man just convicted of the manslaughter of his own daughter—had to say:

> But even after Gloria died, Thomas Sam adhered to his belief that homeopathy was equally valid to conventional medicine for the treatment of eczema.

> He told police: "Conventional medicine would have prolonged her life . . . with more misery. It's not going to cure her and that's what I strongly believe."

He and his wife face 25 years in jail, where they will have plenty of time to rethink their convictions.

[Editor's note: Twenty-five years was the maximum for manslaughter, but the parents had not yet been sentenced at the time this viewpoint was written. Later, the father was sentenced to a minimum of six years and the mother to a minimum of four years.]

The Law Exempting Dietary Supplements from Regulation Should Be Repealed

David H. Gorski

David H. Gorski is a surgical oncologist at the Barbara Ann Karmanos Cancer Institute and an associate professor at Wayne State University. He manages two widely read blogs—one under the pseudonym "Orac"—that are critical of alternative medicine.

Advocates of so-called "complementary and alternative medicine" (CAM) frequently make the claim that they are the victims of a "double standard," in which (or so they claim) they are subjected to harsher standards than what they often refer to as "conventional" or "orthodox" medicine, usually because, don't you know, big pharma controls everything and rigs the game. Whatever the sins of big pharma (and they are legion), this claim is, of course, a whole lot of hooey. If there is a double standard (and, indeed there is), it favors CAM. Indeed, CAM itself is a "wedge strategy" to apply a favorable double standard to modalities that are either ineffective or, although strictly speaking unproven, highly unlikely to be effective based on our understanding of science and prior probability alone. Scientific medicine has to jump through many hoops, including scientific plausibility, biochemical and cell culture studies, animal models, and, finally, randomized clinical trials; in contrast, we are told that we should "respect" CAM modalities and that they should be permitted by "tradition," regardless of whether there's any science whatsoever.

A Double Standard

One area where this double standard is glaringly apparent is in the regulation of supplements by the Food and Drug Administration [FDA]. Among the hodgepodge mishmash of divergent and sometimes mutually contradictory modalities that have found a home under the "big tent" of CAM, there are two areas that come to mind that might actually produce more than placebo effects. The first are herbal medicines, which, being raw plant extracts, are in reality nothing more than impure drugs with variable purity and activity. . . . It's basically the way medicine was practiced a couple of hundred years or more ago, and there really is nothing "alternative" about medicines derived from natural products. Indeed, there is a whole perfectly scientifically respectable field of pharmacology devoted to natural products known as pharmacognosy, whose co-optation as "alternative" by the woo that is CAM is one of the biggest crimes against science ever committed. This second area of CAM that might produce actual effects is the area of dietary supplements, for the same reasons, given that many of them are based on plant extracts. Others, of course, are simply vitamins, all too often taken in much higher doses than ever recommended.

Since 1994, dietary supplements have been almost immune from regulation by the FDA.

Here's where the double standard comes in. Since 1994, dietary supplements have been almost immune from regulation by the FDA, thanks to the Dietary Supplement Health and Education Act of 1994 (DSHEA), which created a new class of regulated entities known as dietary supplements and liberalized the sorts of information that supplement manufacturers could transmit to the public. The end result was:

It [the DSHEA] also expanded the types of products that could be marketed as "supplements." The most logical definition of "dietary supplement" would be something that supplies one or more essential nutrients missing from the diet. DSHEA went far beyond this to include vitamins; minerals; herbs or other botanicals; amino acids; other dietary substances to supplement the diet by increasing dietary intake; and any concentrate, metabolite, constituent, extract, or combination of any such ingredients. Although many such products (particularly herbs) are marketed for their alleged preventive or therapeutic effects, the 1994 law has made it difficult or impossible for the FDA to regulate them as drugs. Since its passage, even hormones, such as DHEA and melatonin, are being hawked as supplements.

For science- and evidence-based medicine, the DSHEA has been an unmitigated disaster.

Indeed, the DSHEA largely allows the use of the "Quack Miranda warning" ["this product is not intended to diagnose, treat, cure or prevent any disease"] to avoid FDA scrutiny. It in essence neutered the FDA, making it very hard for it to regulate so-called dietary supplements, even when potentially dangerous. In brief, it (mostly) exempts from regulation compounds "generally recognized as safe" if they were in widespread use before 1994. While this is reasonable for true foods, such as corn, wheat, or other ingredients, a lot of supplements have pharmacologically active ingredients. Worse, the DSHEA allows manufacturers to make "structure/function" claims. Specifically, the law allows dietary supplements to bear "statements of support" for (a) a benefit for classical nutrient deficiency disease; (b) a description of how ingredients affect the structure or function of the body, organs, or cells; (c) the documented mechanism by which the ingredients act to maintain structure or function; and (d) general well-being from consumption of the ingredients. As Quackwatch.com points out, the statement "calcium builds strong bones and teeth" is a classic example of an allowable structure/function statement for a food.

Unfortunately, supplement manufacturers often go far beyond such uncontroversial statements to claims of curing all sorts of disease, albeit usually in the form of postulated vague benefits, all communicated with a "nudge, nudge, wink, wink" that lets the people buying them know what the *real* health claims are. For science- and evidence-based medicine, the DSHEA has been an unmitigated disaster, although the quacks sure do like it because before a supplement can be removed from the market the burden of proof is on the FDA to show that the supplement is dangerous, not on the manufacturer to show that it's safe, as is the case for drugs. That's one reason why it was so difficult to get ephedra off the market; indeed, it was a decade after the first advisory before the FDA could finally pull ephedra from the market—and then only after thousands of adverse events and several deaths. Can you imagine the reaction that would have occurred if such a delay had occurred for a pharmaceutical product with exactly the same number of adverse events?

A Lucrative Business

In fact, the DSHEA is so much of a problem that even under the [George W.] Bush administration, the Government Accountability Office (GAO) commissioned a report on dietary supplements, which was released in January of this year [2009]. The report, entitled "Dietary Supplements: The FDA Should Take Further Actions to Improve Oversight and Consumer and Understanding" presents evidence of a real problem.

The report begins by pointing out that, since the passage of the DSHEA, dietary supplements have become big business:

Dietary supplements and foods containing added dietary ingredients, such as vitamins and herbs, constitute growing multibillion-dollar industries. Sales of dietary supplements alone reached approximately $23.7 billion in 2007, and data from the 2007 National Health Interview Survey show that over half of all U.S. adults consume dietary supplements. In 1994, there were approximately 4,000 dietary supplement products on the market, whereas an industry source estimated that, in 2008, about 75,000 dietary supplement products were available to consumers. Similarly, food products—such as fortified cereals and energy drinks—that contain added dietary ingredients are in the marketplace in unprecedented numbers, and consumers are expected to spend increasing amounts on these products over the next several years.

Indeed, so lucrative are supplements, and, thanks to the DSHEA, so free from regulation (at least compared to drugs) that increasingly large pharmaceutical companies are muscling in on the action to claim their share of the lucre. In response to the ephedra debacle, as the GAO report points out, a new law was passed called the Dietary Supplement and Nonprescription Drug Consumer Protection Act, which requires companies that receive a serious adverse event report to submit information about the event to FDA beginning in December 2007. This GAO report thus examines such adverse event reports (AERs) from 2007 to January 2009 and was initiated at the request of Representatives Henry A. Waxman, chairman, and John D. Dingell, chairman emeritus, Committee on Energy and Commerce, House of Representatives; Representative Bart Stupak, chairman, Subcommittee on Oversight and Investigations, Committee on Energy and Commerce; and Senator Richard Durbin. This is the CliffsNotes version of the findings:

> Since mandatory reporting requirements went into effect, the agency has seen a threefold increase in the number of all adverse events reported compared with the previous year. For example, from January through October 2008, FDA received 948 adverse event reports, compared with 298 received over the same time period in 2007. Of the 948 adverse event reports, 596 were mandatory reports of serious adverse events submitted by industry; the remaining 352 were voluntary reports, which include all moderate and mild adverse events reported and any serious adverse events

reported by health care practitioners and consumers directly to FDA. However, FDA recently estimated that the actual number of total adverse events—including mild, moderate, and serious—related to dietary supplements per year is over 50,000, which suggests that underreporting of adverse events limits the amount of information FDA receives. To facilitate adverse event reporting for all FDA-regulated products, FDA is currently developing MedWatchPlus, an interactive Web-based portal intended to simplify the reporting process and reduce the time and cost associated with reviewing paper reports.

Nearly 32% of supplement-related AERs resulted in hospitalization between 2003–2008; 13% were life-threatening; and 4% resulted in death.

Moreover, nearly 32% of supplement-related AERs resulted in hospitalization between 2003–2008; 13% were life-threatening; and 4% resulted in death. Possible reasons for the underreporting are described thusly:

Experts have cited several possible reasons for underreporting related to dietary supplements, including reduced attribution of adverse effects to supplements due to the assumption that all dietary supplements are safe, the reluctance of consumers to report dietary supplement use to physicians, the failure to recognize chronic or cumulative toxic effects from their use, and a cumbersome reporting process.

In other words, people assume supplements are safe, and therefore do not routinely associate adverse events that they might have with the supplements. The report also cites a number of problems that hamper the FDA, including limited information about supplements and their manufacturers (or even how many manufacturers there were; the identity of ingredients in the various supplements; and the mild and moderate AERs made to companies. But the worst problem hampering the FDA's ability to protect the public from dubious supplements is that it lacks mandatory recall authority. That's right. The FDA can recall drugs if it decides there is evidence that they are unsafe, but for supplements it has to prove they're unsafe *before* recalling them—yet another double standard favoring CAM. Meanwhile resources for regulating potentially dangerous supplements are tight; the FDA devoted only 1% of its field resources to dietary supplement programs from fiscal years 2006 through 2007.

Recommendations for Action

So what does the GAO recommend? Do you have to ask? There were four recommendations for executive action:

1. To improve the information available to FDA for identifying safety concerns and better enable FDA to meet its responsibility to protect the public health, we recommend that the Secretary of the Department of Health and Human Services direct the Commissioner of FDA to request authority to require dietary supplement companies to

   > identify themselves as a dietary supplement company as part of the existing registration requirements and update this information annually,

   > provide a list of all dietary supplement products they sell and a copy of the labels and update this information annually, and

   > report all adverse events related to dietary supplements.

2. To better enable FDA to meet its responsibility to regulate dietary supplements that contain new dietary ingredients, we recommend that the Secretary of the Department of Health and Human Services direct the Commissioner of FDA to issue guidance to clarify when

an ingredient is considered a new dietary ingredient, the evidence needed to document the safety of new dietary ingredients, and appropriate methods for establishing ingredient identity.

3. To help ensure that companies follow the appropriate laws and regulations and to renew a recommendation we made in July 2000, we recommend that the Secretary of the Department of Health and Human Services direct the Commissioner of FDA to provide guidance to industry to clarify when products should be marketed as either dietary supplements or conventional foods formulated with added dietary ingredients.

4. To improve consumer understanding about dietary supplements . . . , we recommend that the Secretary of the Department of Health and Human Services direct the Commissioner of FDA to coordinate with stakeholder groups involved in consumer outreach to (1) identify additional mechanisms—such as the recent WebMD partnership—for educating consumers about the safety, efficacy, and labeling of dietary supplements; (2) implement these mechanisms; and (3) assess their effectiveness.

These are all reasonable sounding enough, but they are mere Band-Aids on a sucking chest wound. What all this bureaucratese represents is nothing more than an admission that, as long as the DSHEA is in effect, all the FDA can do is whittle around the edges and try to increase consumer outreach efforts to educate the public, clarify what is and is not considered a "supplement," and improve reporting mechanisms to monitor adverse events. The reason, of course, is that that is all the FDA can do as long as the DSHEA is law and the bogus construct of vague "structure/function" claims acts as a shield to protect manufacturers from oversight. Regulations need to be based on science and designed so that the level of evidence required for each type of medicine under consideration is reasonable, based on existing science. It does not have to be "total regulation" (as for new drugs) versus no regulation. Intermediate levels of regulation are possible and would make sense for certain classes of herbal remedies.

Of course, the real answer to the problem is to repeal the DSHEA and replace it with a law that clearly defines what is and is not "food" and eliminates the loophole that allows manufacturers of dubious herbal remedies to add a bit of this amino acid or that vitamin, label their concoction as "food" or a dietary supplement, and thereby hide under the mantle of incredibly weak regulation.

Access to Complementary and Alternative Therapies Must Be Protected

Diane Miller

Diane Miller is an attorney and cofounder of the National Health Freedom Coalition (NHFC).

NHFC [National Health Freedom Coalition] sent communication to the [Barack] Obama administration at Change.gov, emphasizing the importance of health freedom considerations when creating health care policy. . . .

Here is the message sent by NHFC:

My name is Diane Miller and I am an attorney and Director of Law and Public Policy for National Health Freedom Coalition (NHFC) (www.nationalhealthfreedom.org). NHFC annually hosts the United States Health Freedom Assembly, including 45 voting member organizations working to protect health freedom and working to build consensus and solutions for health care.

We have endorsed the International Declaration of Health Freedom passed in 2006 by the World Health Freedom Assembly.

Not only do Americans need access to conventional medical health care without economic barriers, but they need access to whatever type of health care they want, whether it is conventionally medical, or natural and holistic; whether it is preventive or critical care, whether it is from licensed conventional providers, or from practitioners of noninvasive approaches within the community that should not require occupational licensure. We need all hands on deck. One size does not fit all.

Health is a personal journey and Americans need their healing preferences and journey protected. Americans need the economic barriers to conventional care removed, and they need the barriers of access to natural remedies removed and natural healing protected.

NHFC trains leaders on how to be politically active and be advocates for change. There are three areas that health freedom leaders are diligently working on in the health freedom movement for change, State, Federal, and International.

Health is a personal journey and Americans need their healing preferences and journey protected.

---

1. *State law*–a.) The passage of safe harbor exemption laws that protect the right of Americans to access nonmedical health care practitioners who are practicing safely in the public domain without occupational licensing, such as natural, complementary, or alternative forms of healing, homeopathy, herbalism, massage and bodywork, and naturopathy, to enable these practitioners to continue to practice without being criminally charged for practicing medicine without a license, (six states already have passed and 22 more states have introduced these measures) and b.) passage of new laws that allow medical doctors to provide holistic and natural health care solutions without being disciplined or losing their license for going outside of prevailing conventional care (23 states have passed these laws and one state passed a law for all licensed professionals to use complementary and alternative health care).

2. *Federal law–Foods are not drugs.* Introduction of bills that take back the rights of people to make truthful health claims for foods and dietary supplements that are generally regarded as safe, without that food or dietary

supplement automatically legally turning into a drug by definition, thus being the foundation of criminal charges of drug use (the fact that a food legally turns into a drug when used for prevention and cure of disease because of the definition of drug based on intent of use, is outmoded and extremely detrimental to access to nutrients by the American public).

3. *International regulations and guidelines*–Passage of congressional directives to US employees: Americans who represent us at international forums should represent US law and the interests of the people, rather than representing the agendas of the various agencies that employ them. (The FDA [Food and Drug Administration] and US delegates have systematically indicated approval of maximum upper limits on vitamins and minerals for global trade guidelines while representing the US in global forums such as the United Nations Codex Alimentarius, in direct opposition to the . . . 1994 Dietary Supplement Health and Education Act establishing no upper limits on vitamins and minerals.)

Government-Enforced Monopoly

Conventional medical care with drugs and surgery has become the main government-endorsed option for health care in our country because of conventional state occupation laws and federal substance and drug law. All other options, which are often economically sounder and that promote prevention and the vital force of the human body, have been systematically outlawed over the years, leaving us with a "conventional medical drug based monopoly enforced by governments."

Healers and practitioners that choose not to be medical professionals under state licensing laws can be charged criminally in most states for practicing medicine without a license. State licensed medical doctors and professionals cannot wander outside of their conventionally accepted and prevailing standards of care or they are vulnerable to losing their licenses, even though they have secured patient informed consent and no harm has been caused. Both licensed and unlicensed practitioners can be charged under federal law for using unapproved drugs if they use a natural substance (even water) for the prevention and cure of a disease, because the legal definition of drug is based on "intent of use of a substance" rather than whether something is a natural, generally regarded as safe, substance or whether it is a toxic substance.

If we continue to allow the status quo, where licensed physicians are blocked from providing natural therapies, and unlicensed natural healers are criminally charged for practicing medicine without a license, and all practitioners are prohibited from using natural substances for prevention and cure of disease, then for sure we have lost the greatest freedom of all—the freedom to survive on our own terms.

The 2010 Health Care Reform Law Hurts Users of Alternative Therapies

Curt Levey and Jim Turner

Curt Levey, an attorney, is executive director of the Committee for Justice. Jim Turner, also an attorney, is chairman of Citizens for Health.

We are the heads of two nonprofit organizations—one of us liberal and the other conservative—who are concerned that the impending [as of March 2010] healthcare legislation will negatively impact holistic and natural medicine and limit the healthcare choices of the people who consume it.

Because alternative medicine is highly effective in treating many of the chronic conditions which resist treatment by establishment medicine—from arthritis, heart disease, and chronic pain to insomnia and attention deficit disorders— nearly 50 percent of Americans regularly use some type of alternative therapy, according to a study by the *Journal of the American Medical Association*. In fact, the study found that visits to alternative practitioners, for treatments ranging from acupuncture and chiropractic to herbal remedies, outnumber all visits to primary care physicians by almost two to one. Additionally, more than 100 million Americans "regularly consume dietary supplements as a means of improving and maintaining healthy lifestyles," according to a U.S. senator who has worked on related legislation.

Nonetheless, "alternative therapies (including acupuncture, chelation therapy, biofeedback and holistic medicine) are not covered by Medicare," says the federal government. The same is true of Medicaid. Nobody expects better coverage for alternative treatments when, as a key part of the reform legislation, the Department of Health and Human Services (HHS) determines the "essential health benefits" that insurance plans will contain. When supporters of the legislation speak of a right to healthcare, they mean a right to establishment medicine.

When supporters of the [healthcare reform] legislation speak of a right to healthcare, they mean a right to establishment medicine.

Consumers of alternative medicine are used to health insurance plans that offer little or no coverage for holistic treatments and thus don't meet their needs. That's why many of them choose not to purchase health insurance. What they're not used to—but will have to get used to if the proposed "reforms" become law—is being forced to purchase the very insurance plans that fail to meet their needs. And therein lie the dire consequences of the impending legislation.

If you're an alternative healthcare consumer, the money you will be forced to spend subsidizing other people's establishment healthcare, through premiums and higher taxes, is money you can no longer spend on holistic and natural medicine for you and your family. It's as if the government forced you to join and pay for a food shopping club that didn't include natural food stores. After you finished paying thousands of dollars up front to the big supermarket chains you rarely if ever visit, where would you find the money for the natural food you really want?

Sure, you can lobby HHS to include a few alternative treatments as "essential health benefits"—just as you can ask the big supermarket chains to carry some natural foods—but you shouldn't have to beg to spend your money on the type of healthcare you want.

If you don't think you will be affected by the government's forced transfer of healthcare dollars from alternative to establishment medicine, consider the breadth of treatments that will be completely or partially excluded when federal bureaucrats draw up the list of essential benefits. You will be affected if you're one of the patients of America's 70,000 chiropractors, if you use an athletic trainer to treat your sports injury, or if you're a woman who would prefer to give birth at home with the help of a midwife. You'll be affected if you rely on treatments that are a traditional part of your culture or anyone else's culture, whether you seek help from Native American medicine, acupuncture and other traditional Chinese treatments, India's Ayurveda—made famous by physician Deepak Chopra—or the Latin American hueseros and sobadores who treat traumatic and occupational injuries.

Every American deserves the right to make their own healthcare choices with their own healthcare dollars.

Consumers of these indigenous healing traditions are particularly vulnerable to the forced transfer of healthcare dollars because their typically modest incomes will make it difficult to pay for both their traditional medical practitioners and the new federally mandated health insurance premiums. So much for the World Health Organization's (WHO's) recommendation that indigenous medicine be integrated into national healthcare programs. Instead, so many of the American politicians who pay lip service to respect for racial and cultural differences appear ready to hand the feds the power to impose a one-size-fits-all healthcare solution.

In the end, the essential point is not what the WHO recommends or whether acupuncture will be effective in relieving your chronic pain. The point is that every American deserves the right to make their own healthcare choices with their own healthcare dollars. No healthcare system will guarantee you access to every treatment you ever want—not an unregulated free market, not Medicare, not Medicaid, and certainly not "ObamaCare." But when you're allowed the freedom to make your own choices about treatments and insurance plans, you can prioritize what access is most important to you.

We all lose out when those choices are taken away, and not just in the obvious ways. With the impending diversion of money away from alternative medicine, the development of new holistic therapies that could benefit everybody will be stifled. If, instead, the Congress and president chose the path of fostering true competition in the health insurance market, insurance plans that cater more to our varied needs—including the needs of the natural medicine community—would likely bloom and expand. The increase in competition among treatments and insurance plans would put downward pressure on the high cost of establishment medicine, especially because alternative medicine typically has a lower price tag. We would all benefit.

Whether you prefer establishment medicine or are a fan of acupuncture, biofeedback, and dietary supplements, there are good reasons to share our concern about the negative impact of the impending legislation on alternative medicine and healthcare choice in general.

Opponents of CAM Apply a Double Standard to Evidence of Its Effectiveness

Richard A. Jaffe

Richard A. Jaffe is a health care litigator and counselor. He is the author of Galileo's Lawyer: Courtroom Battles in Alternative Health, Complementary Medicine and Experimental Treatments, *from which this viewpoint is taken.*

All clinical or certified nutritionists believe in the healing powers of specific foods, vitamins, supplements and herbal remedies. They are all opposed to an over-reliance on processed or highly refined foods (such as canned foods, frozen dinners, fast food, etc.) to meet dietary needs.

Almost all nutritionists believe that a healthy diet consists mostly of vegetables, legumes, fruits, nuts, some types of fish, chicken (free range if possible), and occasionally, lean cuts of beef, if you can't live without it. However, even with a relatively healthy diet, most nutritionists believe that dietary supplementation is necessary for almost all people because of the poor state of the food supply, the American diet, air and water pollution, and poor farming practices. Many nutritionists provide highly individualized counseling based on a variety of assessments and testing.

Basically, the stock-in-trade of nutritionists is the recommendation of foods and the sale of professional-grade supplements to correct nutritional deficits and resolve medical problems. And that is the biggest bone of contention between nutritionists and the registered dietitians.

The registered dietitians (RDs) are the largest, most organized, and best funded food/nutrition professional group in the country. The RDs believe that only supplements which have been proven to be effective by randomized controlled clinical studies that have been published in a few mainstream medical journals should be recommended to people.

The dietitians believe that at the current time, there are only approximately three supplements that have met this standard: calcium for people with osteoporosis, folic acid for pregnant women, and maybe vitamin D for people with calcium or vitamin D deficiencies. The recommendation by nutrition practitioners of any other supplement for any other condition is considered by the dietitians to be unethical quackery.

It is ironic that when the proven and established medical therapies were leeches, bleeding, and forcing patients to ingest caustics like mercury, the medical establishment was calling other people quacks.

This is complete and utter nonsense and a short digression is needed to explain why.

Just How "Scientific" Is Conventional Medicine?

For hundreds of years, conventional doctors have been complaining about quacks and charlatans who use unproven remedies. It is ironic that when the proven and established medical therapies were leeches, bleeding, and forcing patients to ingest caustics like mercury, the medical establishment was calling other people quacks, including nonmedical-school-trained people who were giving citizens herbs and other folk remedies to treat medical conditions. Does any of this sound familiar?

Fast-forward to 1978. The congressional Office of Technology Assessment [OTA], aided by an advisory board composed of leading medical and university school faculty, published a report entitled "Assessing the Efficacy and Safety of Medical

Technologies." The report estimated that only between ten and twenty percent of all conventional medical therapies have been proven by scientific evidence.

The OTA report caused much hand-wringing among the medical church elders. In response, they invented a new paradigm called "evidence-based medicine" and called for "outcomes research" to justify medical therapeutics. Under the new paradigm, medical interventions were supposed to be based on scientific evidence, and if possible, on the gold standard, which is the randomized, controlled clinical trial.

Since that time there have been a number of studies showing that there are varying degrees of scientific support for a much larger percentage of therapies than the OTA's estimate. However, it seems clear that the majority of medical therapeutics is not supported by primary (as opposed to meta-analyzed) randomized, controlled clinical trials, and there are many other kinds of evidence that medical practitioners rely on daily in making therapeutic decisions. The dietitians' insistence on controlled clinical trials as a prerequisite to recommending a supplement is simply not consistent with the therapeutic practices of contemporary medicine. The dietitians are attempting to hold the nutrition field to a higher standard than the standard primarily used in medical therapeutics.

Laymen do not understand how much bias, subjectivity, professional self-interest, and trade protectionism is involved in the regulation and sanctioning of health practitioners.

The Food Fights

All the professional nutritionist groups and the entire supplement and health food community believe that the scientific and clinical evidence (the same type and quality of evidence relied upon by doctors every day in their therapeutic practices) is very strong for the use of nutritional supplements and herbs for many conditions. They also believe that much of the negative scientific information about supplements is a result of bias and faulty science.

The dietitians think that any nutritionist who sells supplements instead of just giving advice will go straight to hell because of the conflict of interest in both giving advice and selling a product as a result of that advice. (By that logic, any surgeon who actually cuts someone open, rather than just advising surgery, would have the same conflict of interest.)

The nutritionist groups and the alternative health community believe that dietitians are only experts in food technology and that they are unqualified to provide sophisticated, clinical nutritional advice unless they obtain training beyond the dietetics curriculum.

Most ominously, the dietitians believe that only a registered dietitian should be permitted to give advice about nutrition.

During the beginning of a recent Texas legislative session that dealt with the fight between the dietitians and the nutritionists, a legislator was overheard to say, "Here we go again, the food fights." . . .

Balancing Competing Interests

Complementary and alternative practitioners will surely continue to be prosecuted, persecuted, and sued. These battles will continue to be fought so long as people have medical conditions that cannot be cured by conventional medicine—in other words, so long as there continues to be a need or demand for the services and products of complementary and alternative practitioners and manufacturers. . . .

Many of the cases in this field involve two competing interests or policies: the right of people to have control over their own bodies versus the government's role or obligation to protect the public from dangerous, questionable, or unproven remedies. Most reasonable people would agree that both interests are legitimate. So it becomes a matter of balancing these competing interests.

The clearest example of where the government overprotects people is in its irrational insistence that terminally ill cancer patients should only use FDA [Food and Drug Administration]-approved drugs or standard remedies and can only use experimental drugs after so-called "proven remedies" have failed. Everyone in the conventional medical community knows that there are certain types of cancer for which there are no conventional curative treatments. The FDA's insistence that terminal patients take these drugs (which at best extend life a few weeks or a month or two) before experimental or unconventional treatment can be utilized makes no sense.

For over a dozen years, legislators like Senator Tom Harkin and Congressman Dan Burton have tried to fix this problem. But their legislation has gone nowhere ultimately because the medical and pharmaceutical industries do not support it, and most Congress folk are not interested in protecting the average person from government in this area, or so it would seem to me. A new access bill is now circulating, and maybe this time Congress will do the right thing.

Even the courts have tried to create an exemption from the FDA act for terminally ill cancer patients. In the 1970s, a brave Oklahoma district court judge tried to give people the constitutional or statutory right to use unconventional medicine like laetrile, but the Supreme Court slapped him down. Just recently, a panel of the District of Columbia Federal Court of Appeals suggested that terminally ill patients may have a right to investigational drugs before their approval. However, on reargument before all the judges of the circuit, the case was reversed. So terminally ill patients are still left with only FDA-approved treatments. This just seems wrong to me. Dying patients should have the ultimate say as to what treatment they should be able to take, and their choices should include any experimental or unconventional treatment the patients can get their hands on.

Information Must Be Accurate

But on the other hand, I don't have a problem with state governments prosecuting naturopaths or anyone else who pretends they are doctors, who vastly inflate their credentials, or who scare people into taking supplements to cure "tendencies" to cancer. And of course, above all else, information about drugs, supplements, products and devices, and testing equipment should be as accurate and complete as possible, on pain of unwanted governmental attention. There should be little tolerance for anyone, whether conventional or complementary, who misleads the public or patients, or overstates their qualifications, experience or past results.

I have a major problem with the undereducated but well-organized and well-financed dietitians who are trying to stop the dissemination of truthful information about dietary supplements and who pretend there is not a vast body of literature out there supporting the use of many supplements. This smacks of the feudal times when guilds protected the monopoly of their members by having the king enforce the guild's exclusive right to practice a trade. That an organization like the dietitians is taking control of the flow of information about nutrition is disconcerting because they are overtly hostile to dietary supplements and oppose efforts to move away from their antiquated "four food group" mentality. Hopefully the success the dietitians have had in the state legislatures will eventually be seen for what it is: a naked grab for power, thinly disguised in the mantle of consumer protection.

I also have a problem with the way drugs are tested in this country. There is too much emphasis on protecting the public, which is an abstract concept, and not enough concern by the government and the drug testing centers on the individual patients/subjects, especially those with terminal diseases.

And it seems to me that there is a fundamental flaw in the way supplements are tested here. Supplements are not drugs and supplements often work differently and more indirectly than drugs. I have seen the way alternative remedies are tested in this country, and I am very skeptical of the methodologies employed. Increasingly, legitimate scientists are starting to publish articles about the bias and methodological flaws in the testing of herbs and supplements.

Lack of Objectivity

Medical science is a human endeavor. That means it is necessarily infused with an inherent disorder, messiness, bias, animus, and lack of objectivity. The philosophers of science have it wrong to the extent they believe that psychology, sociology, prejudice, and even sociopathology play no role in the growth of medical knowledge (or the lack thereof).

As to the legislative and administrative process for the licensing and disciplining of health care practitioners, I think laymen do not understand how much bias, subjectivity, professional self-interest, and trade protectionism is involved in the regulation and sanctioning of health practitioners. Complementary practitioners continue to be sanctioned across the country merely because they use treatments that are not accepted by conventional medicine, even in the absence of patient harm or patient complaints. Some (but certainly not all) of these cases are the result of narrow-minded bias or worse.

Since all of these nonobjective, knowledge-inhibiting, and all-too-human forces will surely continue, the future should be as interesting as the past has been.

People Have a Right to Make Their Own Health Care Choices Even if They Are Wrong

Jon Rappoport

Jon Rappoport is an investigative reporter and consultant. He has appeared as a guest on more than two hundred radio and television programs.

Since individual freedom has become an endangered species, we need to look at the propaganda that continues to erode freedom.

In particular, we must understand that so-called science and scientific evidence are being used to propagate the view that those who hold "the truth" in their hands have the right to force everyone else to go along.

Nowhere is this clearer than in the field of medical practice.

Against the secret and concealed background of 106,000 annual deaths in America, as a result of the effects of pharmaceutical drugs, public health agencies continually tell us they know what's best for our health. Why? Because they are relying on good science about disease, diagnosis, and treatment.

We, the great unwashed public, know nothing. We couldn't know anything, because we haven't done the research, we haven't read the studies, we wouldn't be able to comprehend the studies even if we could find them.

So, based on what science, precisely, do we get, as an outcome, 106,000 deaths in the US, every year, from the effects of government-approved medical drugs?

Reporters never pose that question to public health agencies.

The presumption is, if you know the truth, you have the right to force people to toe the line of that truth. In other words, they have no right to be wrong.

"We're the experts. We just diagnosed you with RFTYX-45, a dangerous condition that could result in the disintegration of your spleen and liver. We've written the prescription for AbbaDabba, the only drug that could reverse this condition. You're refusing the drug, and you're opting, instead, to drink a tea made from dirt. You're obviously insane."

Does the patient have the right to eat dirt?

Let's make it more severe. Does the patient have the right to chew tobacco to cure his illness?

Does the patient have the right to stand on his head in a snowstorm, naked, to cure his illness?

Does he have the right to lean up against a liquor store window and chant verses of regulations from the alcohol control board manual, in order to heal himself?

Does he have the right to sleep in a garbage bin for a month to cure himself?

Does he have the right to jump off a hundred-foot cliff to rid himself of his illness?

And the answer is yes. He has that right. He is free to choose.

If the vast social and political agenda aimed at coercing people into "accepting help" wins out, freedom is gone.

The Patient's Right to Be Wrong

It's not a question of who has the best science, or who can present the best lies about having science. That question, when it comes right down to it, is irrelevant.

We have to understand this.

On the other side of the coin, you see, is the proposition that the government exists to protect everybody, everywhere, all the time. And when you choose to enter that door, you give up your freedom.

The entire "sympathy industry" is built to allow "the experts" to help victims by, in essence, telling them what they must do. That industry was also built to promote the gooey idea of an eternally meddling community of concerned people who descend on the rest of us, and advise us about our choices.

There are many reasons for freedom, and one of them is: You ultimately follow your own counsel and judgment, and you accept the consequences. You don't just do this once, you do it all your life. It's a road you walk.

If the vast social and political agenda aimed at coercing people into "accepting help" wins out, freedom is gone.

We have been taught that every weird action a person takes, every strange choice he makes, every odd idea he voices has an explanation . . . and if we can dig up that explanation, we will understand how and why the person departed from the group and the norm and the acceptable path. And then we can place a label on the person. We can decide "he needs help."

This approach has been taken to such an extreme that many of us no longer really believe in that person's freedom. Instead, we think he is simply a slave to some distorted inner impulse, and we should do what we can to root out that impulse and return the person to sanity.

On this battlefield, freedom becomes the casualty and the sacrifice. But of course we don't recognize this. We're so busy trying to fix and patch and rebuild, we lose the thread.

Government does the same thing, except its attitude is cynical and manipulative. Its day of paradise will come when the entire population is convinced that endless official help is necessary for survival. Then the beneficent authority can carve up the human psyche into regions that respond to the stimulation of "gifts."

Freedom and choice will become relics of a long-gone past.

"Oh, yes. That dinosaur came and went. Now we have share and care. We're really human in this day and age. And we have the science to prove it. Have you seen the recent study that was published by . . . ?"

CHAPTER 4

What Complementary Therapies Are Used with Conventional Medicine?

Chapter Preface

In addition to therapies from established alternative medicine systems that are also used as complementary therapies, there are many that are only complementary—that is, they are not used alone but are always additions to conventional medicine or some other system. A few such complementary therapies are uncontroversial, except in regard to disagreement about how worthwhile they are. For example, art therapy, music therapy, meditation, and tai chi are rarely if ever viewed as foolish or harmful, although not everyone believes that they are of value in treatment of illness. Some others, however, are strongly criticized by medical professionals and science advocates who consider them potentially harmful and at best a waste of time and money.

At its website, the American Cancer Society lists the following complementary therapies as worth considering. It does not, of course, mean that any of these things can cure cancer—only that they may help to relieve symptoms or make a person feel better emotionally.

- Acupuncture (insertion of thin needles into the body at specific points).

- Aromatherapy (use of fragrant substances to improve mood).

- Art therapy (expression of emotions through creative activities).

- Biofeedback (a method of helping people learn to control unconscious processes).

- Labyrinth walking (meditative walking along winding pathways laid out on the ground).

- Massage therapy (rubbing of the body's soft tissue).

- Meditation (using concentration or reflection to relax the body and calm the mind).

- Music therapy (the use of music to promote emotional healing).

- Tai chi (an ancient martial art now used for health that involves movement and breathing).

- Yoga (a form of non-aerobic exercise involving precise postures).

Prayer and spirituality are also included on the list, but while prayer is widely acknowledged to help in coping with illness, most people today do not view it as a complementary therapy. R. Barker Bausell writes in his book *Snake Oil Science: The Truth About Complementary and Alternative Medicine*, "I wouldn't classify people who pray for relief of a symptom or deliverance from a disease as CAM [complementary and alternative medicine] users because prayer isn't a medical (i.e., physical, mental, chemical, or psychic) intervention." On the other hand, traditional healing rituals such as those of Native American or African cultures do employ prayer as a means of curing illness.

Another concept that can cause confusion about the scope of CAM is "mind/body medicine." Although this is one of the categories into which CAM therapies are divided, the term is not applied exclusively to CAM. A growing number of researchers and conventional doctors use the term "mind/body medicine" in recognizing the effect of the mind on physiological processes, whether or not they endorse any complementary therapies.

Besides the above complementary therapies, there are many less widely used ones such as qigong (which is similar to tai chi), guided imagery, hypnotherapy, and a variety of movement therapies, as well as dog therapy for help with emotional problems. Energy-based therapies—for example magnet therapy, Reiki, and healing touch—are viewed less favorably by science advocates than most of the others, since these therapies depend on the unproven premise that undetectable energy fields affect the body and in some cases can be transmitted by the hands of one person to another. Many consider this pseudoscience and therefore deceptive, while others feel that it is harmless and may be helpful to people who believe in it.

The complementary therapies to which conventional medicine raises the strongest objections are those that involve drastically imbalanced diets or the consumption of exceptionally large amounts of supplements or other substances. If these are relied on exclusively, they may delay standard treatment; moreover, some are harmful in themselves. "Certain vitamins and minerals can increase the risk of cancer or other illnesses, especially if too much is taken," states the American Cancer Society, and "some alternative biological therapies are no less toxic than chemotherapy."

Because so many different complementary therapies exist, and there are so many practitioners—qualified and unqualified—of each, no blanket statement can be made about their value. It is safe to say, however, that claims of complete cure by any single form of therapy should be viewed with suspicion.

Tai Chi Has Many Health Benefits for People of All Ages and Conditions

HealthyWomen

HealthyWomen is a website containing current information about medical and health issues that affect women.

A technique that integrates body, mind and spirit, tai chi (pronounced *tie-chee*) has been practiced for centuries in China. Tai chi means "grand ultimate" and implies "the balance of opposing forces of nature." The traditional training is intended to teach awareness of one's own balance, both physical and mental.

Tai chi began as a martial art, but today it's most frequently practiced for its health benefits and meditative properties. It has become a popular exercise for millions of Chinese and is especially popular among older people.

Tai chi was introduced to the United States in the mid 1960s. Now it's hard to find an exercise center that doesn't offer classes. People all over the world practice tai chi every day.

In tai chi, you perform a series of slow, graceful, controlled body movements while your body remains straight and upright. It includes stepping, shifting weight and rotating. Throughout the session, your breathing becomes deep, yet relaxed. Tai chi movements have been compared to those performed in yoga and ballet.

Stories abound about the origins of tai chi. According to one of the most popular legends, tai chi's motions are based on those of a snake. A martial arts master named [Zhang] Sanfeng dreamed about a battle between a snake and a crane during which he noted the snake's graceful fighting movements. Those movements inspired the development of the noncombative style of tai chi.

Tai chi is a low-impact activity. One key principle (which comes from Taoism) is wu-wei (or the action of nonaction), which refers to going with the flow—not forcing things.

The Concept of Chi

Like acupuncture, tai chi is based on the concept of chi (pronounced *chee*), the vital life energy that sustains health and calms the mind. Chi courses through your body through specific pathways or meridians. The traditional explanation is that the practice of tai chi improves health by improving the flow of chi, thereby restoring energy balance.

Chi must flow freely for good health; blocked chi can lead to illness or disease. All forms of traditional Chinese medicine (TCM) aim to restore energy balance and conserve the body's chi or life vitality. This health system includes the practices of acupuncture, massage, herbal medicine and tai chi's sister healing art, qigong (pronounced *chee gong*).

Unlike many types of exercise, tai chi is accessible to people of any age and condition—children, senior citizens and even people who use walkers.

Modern researchers are finding amazing health benefits from tai chi. Regular practice builds strength; enhances muscle tone and circulation; and improves balance, flexibility, posture, coordination and range of motion. Some studies also show that tai chi can lower blood pressure and heart rate, as well as ease arthritis pain. It can also help prevent osteoporosis, making it particularly beneficial to women, and reduce the incidence of falls. In addition, tai chi reduces stress, improves concentration and increases energy.

Unlike many types of exercise, tai chi is accessible to people of any age and condition—children, senior citizens and even people who use walkers. It requires no special clothes or equipment, and it can easily be practiced at home. Some modified forms of tai chi can be practiced by individuals with limited mobility. In fact, tai chi is particularly beneficial to the elderly and people with impaired motor skills. Because tai chi emphasizes correct posture and balance, the exercise may be a safer alternative for women with frail bones than other physical activities.

Medical science remains unclear about exactly how tai chi works. While several studies have documented its benefits, none have completely explained why or how it works—at least in the context of Western medicine. But there are theories. While traditional practitioners might attribute the health benefits to the free flow of chi, Western-world scientific research into tai chi is finding other possible explanations for its beneficial effects. For instance:

- Deep breathing promotes relaxation, stress reduction and concentration.

- Focused attention not only relaxes the body and mind, it helps cultivate mental alertness.

- The exercises strengthen muscles and bones. (For instance, as a weight-bearing exercise that requires you to support your weight while standing, tai chi is a good preventive measure for osteoporosis.)

- Since most of the movements involve alternating weight-bearing in the legs, tai chi helps cultivate better balance by improving coordination and control of the body during movements.

Anyone Can Benefit

Anyone can benefit from tai chi—like most low-impact exercises, it can be an important part of a healthy lifestyle. Tai chi isn't a treatment or a cure, but health care professionals often suggest it as a complementary therapy for many conditions.

Few randomized controlled studies (the scientific standard for determining treatment efficacy) have so far been conducted to establish the direct medical benefits of tai chi, however, although some preliminary studies suggest that tai chi can help relieve the symptoms of or prevent certain conditions. Tai chi is considered useful in:

- Reducing the risk of falls in the elderly by improving balance and strength as well as confidence.

- Improving cardiopulmonary function.

- Reducing blood pressure.

- Reducing stress.

- Helping to strengthen the muscles around an arthritic joint, improving flexibility and range of motion while reducing joint pain. Stronger muscles also help protect the joint from soft tissue injuries.

- Easing back pain by improving flexibility.

- Slowing the decline in respiratory function, often a concern among the elderly. Plus, the regular exercise afforded by the practice—comparable to a low-impact aerobic workout—provides cardiorespiratory conditioning.

- Stimulating circulation, improving blood flow to the extremities and its return to the heart.

- Improving health-related quality of life in the elderly.

- Helping speed recovery after a heart attack. Tai chi is sometimes used as an adjunct therapy in cardiac rehabilitation. One reason for its benefit may be its ability to reduce blood pressure and heart rate.

- Helping people with multiple sclerosis increase their physical activity and functioning by enhancing muscle tone, flexibility, coordination and general well-being. Some chapters of the National Multiple Sclerosis Society now offer tai chi classes.

- Helping to slow or prevent bone loss since it's a weight-bearing exercise.

- Reducing the amount of stress hormones in the body.

- Improving glucose control in people with type 2 diabetes.

It's important to remember, however, that although tai chi may help prevent and manage a number of conditions, it isn't a cure for anything.

Music Therapy Is
Used in Many Ways to
Help Patients Heal

Pam Mellskog

Pam Mellskog is a health reporter who lives in Colorado.

Betsey Carle never autographs napkins, wears sequined gowns, or takes tips.

But the music therapist, who follows a "professional casual" dress code, is every bit as interested as the stage performer in connecting with her audience. Carle's audience just happens to include psychiatric and hospice patients at Adventist Medical Center in Portland, Oregon.

One day while Carle was on the job an elderly hospice patient with faltering memory gave her a snippet of a lyric from an old song he longed to hear but could not place.

Carle searched her songbooks for four months to finally identify and sing "When It's Springtime in the Rockies" while strumming her guitar.

"The music made a difference," Carle says. "Many people in that age group remember the song. They mouth the words. And because music is tied into emotion, cognition, and memory in the brain, it takes them back to a more normal time," she says. "That's healing."

The Science of Music

Music therapists hope that scientific research continues to define how their work differs from entertainment, and how it benefits patients as much as other more familiar complementary therapies such as art therapy.

Pam Mellskog, "The Sounds of Healing," *Vibrant Life*, vol. 25, November–December 2009, pp. 14–17. All rights reserved. Reproduced by permission.

Even without definitive research, intensive care unit staff at Adventist Bolingbrook Hospital in Bolingbrook, Illinois, recently began using 12 Stryker critical care beds equipped with onboard sound therapy—an aspect of music therapy.

Speakers on either side of the headboard amplify an extensive play list that includes the sounds of bottlenose dolphins and a version of "Ave Maria."

"But it's not a radio," said Kathy Mitchell, chief nursing officer at Bolingbrook. "We believe it's going to make patients more comfortable and reduce the need for medication."

Anthropological studies show that music has been used as a healing agent since the earliest times. The Bible also documents its restorative power. For instance, when King Saul suffered from a tormenting spirit, he asked David to play the harp. "Then Saul would feel better, and the tormenting spirit would go away," reads 1 Samuel 16:23 (NLT [New Living Translation]).

Music therapists hope that scientific research continues to define how their work differs from entertainment.

However, the intuitive belief of music as a therapy wasn't put into clinical practice until after World War I, according to the American Music Therapy Association. At that time, hospital workers noticed the healing influence of music when visiting musicians played for troops recovering from physical and psychological trauma.

In 2000, Cheryl Dileo, a music therapy professor at Temple University, launched one of the most ambitious studies to measure the effects of music therapy. She reviewed 183 studies published since 1963 that involved more than 8,000 subjects. She found that music therapy was effective in decreasing aggression in Alzheimer's patients and relieving pain in cancer patients.

In his best-selling book *The Mozart Effect*, Don Campbell, a faculty member at the University of Colorado at Boulder's American Music Research Center (AMRC), describes how music can reduce stress, depression, and anxiety; induce relaxation and sleep; activate the body; and improve memory and awareness. Campbell's work extends the investigations of Alfred Tomatis, who in the 1950s experimented using Mozart's music to stimulate children with speech and communication disorders.

Music can reduce stress, depression, and anxiety; induce relaxation and sleep; activate the body; and improve memory and awareness.

Mozart wrote more than 600 major compositions, and something about his music stimulates the brain, according to researchers at the University of California at Irvine who also studied the Mozart effect.

In 2007, at the AMRC's fifth Susan Porter Symposium on Music and Health in America, Campbell acknowledged that some people still view music therapy with skepticism.

"It's because we live in such a noisy world," he says. "One hundred years ago, sound was always potent." TVs, cell phones, video games, and air conditioners have cluttered the soundscape, Campbell says.

The Rhythms of Life

The hospital setting helps quiet the environment, and that's necessary for therapeutic work, says Maria Brignola, coordinator of the Counseling and Therapy Department at Portland's Adventist Medical Center.

According to Brignola, music encourages recovery because it mirrors life-giving biological rhythms such as the heartbeat.

"It's comforting because it's within us," she says. "Most people, if not all, have the ability to relate to it. Music is a universal language."

The benefits of music therapy, Brignola explains, cannot be accurately evaluated through linear analyses. "Healing is not linear. It's more of a spiral. And for full healing to occur, [music therapy] needs to integrate the body and the mind and the whole person."

Music therapist Betsey Carle is certified through the American Music Therapy Association in Silver Spring, Maryland, which represents the gold standard in music therapy training. The association offers a music therapy curriculum that includes a required 1,200-hour internship, proficiency in three instruments, and a national board exam.

Carle not only plays all of the instruments in her push cart—hand drum, keyboard, percussion instruments, guitar, and CD player—she also asks patients to play them. In fact, her guitar comes with a function that performs all the fret-work of specific songs—such as Eric Clapton's "Tears in Heaven"—while someone strums along.

Some nonverbal psychiatric patients experience musical success this way, Carle says. "For psychotic patients who may not be able to articulate their feelings, this is a door that opens through music because it taps into emotions and experiences, and that doesn't have to be explained in words," Carle explains.

Nonverbal hospice patients also respond well to music, according to Carle. She remembers visiting a man in his 90s whose body had become severely contracted due to Parkinson's disease. When Carle visited him, an aid was trying unsuccessfully to feed him. "He had his face screwed up as if to say, 'No one is going to get food past my lips,'" Carle remembers.

Carle reviewed his medical chart and, when she realized his roots as a Hawaiian native, she began her therapy by playing "My Little Grass Shack" and the "Hawaiian Wedding Song" in her guitar's ukulele setting.

"By the end of the session, his face had relaxed. I felt that the music had taken him from a very stubborn place and moved him into a more comfortable and relaxed state," Carle says. "I call these holy moments, and they happen often enough for me to consider music therapy more of a calling than a profession."

Creative Arts Are Often Used as Therapy by Health Care Institutions

Elaine Zablocki

Elaine Zablocki is a medical writer and editor who contributes regularly to many health care publications.

In recent years, hospitals and health systems have used a wide range of nonclinical therapies to help patients heal, including visual arts, poetry, dance, music and drama. Surveys conducted in 2004 and 2007 by the Joint Commission, in partnership with the Society for the Arts in Healthcare, found that about half of healthcare institutions in the United States provide such services, however more study of creative therapy's effectiveness and potential benefits is needed.

"State of the Field Report: Arts in Healthcare" in 2009 found there is a growing body of research linking the arts to improved quality of care, "although much of the research on the economic benefits of arts in healthcare is anecdote-rich, and more quantitative data is needed." The report calls for research on outcomes and financial returns.

Many organizations find arts therapies can yield significant improvements in patients' functioning and systematically incorporate them within other therapeutic programs, particularly behavioral health. For example, the PeaceHealth Medical Group relies on an art therapist, a dance therapist and a poetry therapist to support the Sacred Heart inpatient psychiatric hospital in Eugene, Ore.

"Our focus here is on recovery," says Dale Smith, director of behavioral health for the region. "Over the years, we have learned that when people feel closed off due to an illness such as schizophrenia or bipolar disorder, it is very difficult for them to express what they are experiencing. Since they can't express it clearly, they often act out in ways that are misunderstood or even dangerous."

Poetry and art have been particularly valuable in the unit, she says, since so many clients are troubled by a thought disorder or auditory hallucination, and find it difficult to speak openly. Poetry, for example, gives them a way to focus and form their words and thoughts.

"It gives them a voice," Smith says. "Once they're able to express themselves through drawing or the written word, then they're able to embrace their recovery."

Arts therapies can yield significant improvements in patients' functioning.

Deborah Sadowsky, a certified art therapist who works in the unit, also coordinates a series of three-hour group sessions for outpatients dealing with chronic severe pain. They are referred to the program by local physicians, physical therapists and mental health counselors.

"These groups are an opportunity for people to deal with the experience of chronic pain," she says. "Creating images that embody their experiences can be empowering."

The eight-week program is currently funded by a grant from the Sacred Heart Medical Center Foundation, an affiliate of PeaceHealth. Meetings include education on how to manage pain, visualization and relaxation training, as well as expressive art therapy, Sadowsky says.

Images created by members of the group were exhibited at the state capitol. One, a figure in blue and green, created by an older woman with polymyalgia [rheumatica], expresses how her body feels pain. Another member of the group, asked to describe her experience, created an abstract image she titled "Broken."

"Many people who develop chronic pain struggle with the loss of their self-identity as they deal with the impact on their lives, including a loss of careers, relationships, and functional abilities," Sadowsky says. "The images allow us to become witnesses who understand and acknowledge their experience."

Evidence and Best Practices

While the personal stories are interesting, the focus of healthcare today centers on evidence-based therapies. Although it's still an emerging field, how much evidence is there currently to demonstrate the effectiveness of art therapies?

A review article published in the February 2010 issue of the *American Journal of Public Health* summarizes the results of several studies. For example, a randomized controlled trial of patients with coronary artery disease found improvements in apical heart rates and peripheral temperatures in groups that received relaxation training and music therapy.

A randomized controlled trial of creative visual arts in breast cancer patients found improved well-being and decreased negative emotions. A randomized controlled trial of theater arts in elderly adults also found improvements in cognitive measures.

However, according to authors Heather L. Stuckey and Jeremy Nobel, MD, "As a result of the wide range of studies examining the relationship between multiple varieties of art-related interventions and a similarly large group of physiological and behavioral outcomes, comparisons both between intervention types and within certain disease states or conditions are challenging."

Moreover, many of the studies were observational in nature. They conclude that despite methodological and other limitations, the studies included in the review "appear to indicate that creative engagement can decrease anxiety, stress and mood disturbances."

Dr. Nobel, a researcher in healthcare delivery system design on the faculty of the Harvard School of Public Health, and a published poet, is the founder of the Foundation for Art & Healing. The organization seeks to increase research, expand general awareness of art and healing, and sponsor collaborations between medicine and art.

Under the Behavioral Umbrella

Joan Phillips, president of the American Art Therapy Assn., operates an outpatient family therapy private practice in Norman, Okla. Out of the 26 clients she sees in a typical week, 20 are paid for by some form of managed care, including TRICARE, Blue Cross Blue Shield plans and other commercial payers.

"I am approved based on my years of experience and the various licenses I hold," she says. "However, in my opinion, customer satisfaction with my work is very much based on the art therapy."

Phillips notes that many art therapists hold master's-level behavioral health licenses, and based on that, they are added to managed care panels.

"However, at present, any counselor could say they are doing art therapy. Since the panels don't ask for credentials to back up that claim, there may be some art therapy currently carried out by untrained clinicians," she says.

She would like to see MCOs [managed care organizations] provide reimbursement for coded art therapy services and ask for evidence of board certification when they credential practitioners. MCOs providing reimbursement for complementary/alternative treatments often use the service as a marketing tool.

Trained to Heal

The National Coalition of Creative Arts Therapies Associations, founded in 1979, is an alliance of professional organizations focused on advancing the arts as therapeutic modalities. It represents 15,000 members of six creative therapy associations, including art therapy, dance/movement therapy, drama therapy, music therapy, poetry therapy, and psychodrama. Each association has established professional training and certification standards.

Each creative arts therapist is trained in therapeutic skills, in addition to a particular artistic discipline. For example, dance therapists are trained to use movement as an assessment tool, an intervention, and a means of connection, according to Christina Devereaux, a spokesperson for the American Dance Therapy Assn.

"We use movement to intervene, which means we may assist clients in expanding their repertoire and range of movements," she says.

Psychiatric and depressive disorders have shown upward trends in recent years, calling for the exploration of new, effective therapies that might provide enough evidence for coverage consideration or funding sources.

Each creative arts therapist is trained in therapeutic skills, in addition to a particular artistic discipline.

Jane Schroeder DeSouza, has worked for 30 years at St. Vincent's Hospital, Westchester, which specializes in psychiatric and chemical dependency problems. Patients use art therapy to change behavioral patterns.

For example, DeSouza might ask the group to draw what happens when they get trapped in a pattern of anger. The creative expression reinforces awareness, because they often can visualize actions better than they can verbalize them.

DeSouza says she sees significant improvement from arts therapies, including one patient who recovered well enough to begin looking for a job.

The Arts in Medicine

Shands HealthCare, a major referral hospital affiliated with the University of Florida, began a creative arts program in 1990. Artists from the community volunteer in critical-care areas to engage patients in creative arts to reduce the stress of hospitalization, says Tina Mullen, director of Arts in Medicine at Shands.

The hospital partners with professional artists who are not therapists, and their work does not have a specific diagnostic or rehabilitative objective. At present, the program includes 14 artists in residence, plus 150 art student volunteers. Over the years, hundreds of artists have volunteered their talents for patients' benefit, with Shands HealthCare funding the program.

"It reaches patients and staff in measurable ways, and has value for the organization," Mullen says. "What the arts in healthcare do for an organization, and especially an organization of our size, is bring us back to the human level."

Shands currently sponsors Dance for Life: Movement Program for People with Parkinson's Disease. Professional and student dancers offer 12 weekly sessions for Parkinson's patients treated by the University of Florida's Center for Movement Disorders and Neurorestoration, which is charting the results.

"There is something about the combined impulse of dance and music that is hard to describe," Mullen says. "It leads to improved physical mobility. It leads to joy."

Dog Therapy Helps People Recover from Emotional Illness

Jennifer Caprioli

Jennifer Caprioli is a civilian writer for the US Army at Fort Huachuca, Arizona.

For over 40 years Ken Costich, a former Army colonel, has dealt with post-traumatic stress disorder [PTSD] symptoms.

Lucien Mason, a former lance corporal in the Marine Corps has also coped with PTSD since he returned from Vietnam, more than 35 years ago.

Both men have endured medical treatment and sought psychological assistance from professionals, and both men are turning to service dogs as a last resort.

According to the National Institute of Mental Health, PTSD is an "anxiety disorder that can develop after exposure to a terrifying event or ordeal in which physical harm occurred or was threatened."

"With all the great care Veterans Affairs has given me, they have not been able to find a medication for anger, depression, anxiety or the nightmares that worked for me," Costich explained.

"Medication works 50 percent of the time. Talk therapy, alone, works 30 percent of the time, and dogs work 84.5 percent of the time," said Alicia Miller, Army veteran and co-founder of Operation Wolfhound. "The dogs are proven effective. It's a much better deal for the veteran because they don't have to worry about the side effects of medication."

Jennifer Caprioli, "Dogs Go the Distance," *US Army*, March 4, 2010. www.army.mil. As first appeared in the Fort Huachuca *Scout*.

Operation Wolfhound

Operation Wolfhound began about two years ago when Miller's daughter, Rhiannon, suggested they donate two of their Borzoi puppies to people in need of a service dog. Miller, who also experiences symptoms associated with PTSD, said the dogs were well received and proved to be helpful to their owners. To date, Operation Wolfhound has donated or pledged seven dogs to veterans with PTSD.

Borzoi pups were chosen because of their ability to think independently and be protective without being aggressive. They have the potential to live up to 15 years, and are quiet, large dogs that are able to physically support a person.

Operation Wolfhound puts strict parameters on service dog candidates. For instance, they will not accept a dog that is more than 4 years old.

A dog receives at least 50 hours of training before going to live with their veteran.

Miller also said all dogs must come from parents that were screened for genetic diseases and temperament, usually back four generations. The reason is that a person with PTSD, who is emotionally vulnerable, would not deal well with an early death of their service animal.

The dog and training are provided to the veteran, at no cost. Miller notes that this is important because an adult service dog candidate with basic training would cost the veteran about $5,000 and the training would add up to $40,000.

A dog receives at least 50 hours of training before going to live with their veteran, which is required by the International Association of Assistance Dog Partners [IAADP]. IAADP is a nonprofit organization that represents people partnered with guide, hearing and service dogs.

During this training, the dog is evaluated for temperament, trained to be safe with all other animals and small children, and introduced to many public situations.

"You never know what the veteran's situation is going to be so you train for every situation," Miller explained.

After a dog receives the minimum training and the trainer feels the canine is ready to serve their veteran, they will hand the Borzoi over to the veteran, and begin weekly hour-long training sessions. The veteran must also work with their dog daily.

"We train the veteran to train the dog the rest of the way, for their specific needs," Miller said, explaining there are two reasons for this method.

A prime candidate for a service dog is a veteran of any war or military armed services who has anxiety disorder, PTSD, or psychological issues that need support.

"When the dog's life span is over the veteran already has the tools to train another dog, and it gives the veteran more control over their condition, meaning, when you're training a dog to take care of your problems you're directly affecting your situation and that makes a big difference."

During their weekly sessions, veterans learn to be in control of the dog by using positive reinforcement.

"This type of training takes longer but it's a bond of complete trust and love when you're done," Miller explained. According to Miller, a prime candidate for a service dog is a veteran of any war or military armed services who has anxiety disorder, PTSD, or psychological issues that need support.

Emotional Support

"There are two types of dogs," she noted, "an emotional support, which can be any breed of dog, and a service, which are used to reduce the symptoms of PTSD and soothe anxiety."

She said the Borzoi breed is not very obedient, but they are empathic. They can be trained to serve various functions, such as reminding their owner to take medications, or calming them down while driving in vehicular traffic.

"They will try to calm their veteran down in an upsetting situation, or will get their owner out of that situation."

Costich, who has been accompanied by Bandit for a month, said it took about three days for the pair to form a bond.

"This dog [did] more for me in three weeks than any medication any doctor has every prescribed," Costich explained. "He senses when I'm having nightmares, and will wake me up [by nuzzling] me."

Bandit has also been able to sense panic attacks. He warns Costich by jumping up, giving him a "hug" and nuzzling him until he gets through it. He has also been able to use Bandit as a crutch for balance.

He says Bandit has become a huge part of him.

"I kind of feel guilty dragging him around with me all over the place but he doesn't seem to mind. He's like my best friend," Costich explained, noting, his wife calls him "my other wife."

Mason, who met his service dog, Corona, for the first time Feb. 20, [2010] said he hopes the dog will help with nightmares associated with PTSD.

"The dog will be able to either lick [my] face or turn the light on to wake [me] up," he explained. And hopes Corona can assist with his road rage.

Since he has high blood pressure, the dog will be trained to sense when he is getting stressed out and will put his head on Mason's lap to be petted, which will aid in calming him down.

Mason has high aspirations for Corona and hopes he will ultimately help reduce the amount of medication he takes. Miller believes Operation Wolfhound has proved to be successful but they constantly face challenges associated with transporting Borzoi dogs from pledges to trainers and veterans.

"We rely on donated rides and do not take [monetary] donations," she said, noting that might change but for right now they are able to keep Operation Wolfhound a success through volunteers and dogs donated by Borzoi Club of America members. Over 100 volunteers, throughout the United States and Canada, contribute their time to Operation Wolfhound.

She said they also rely heavily on word-of-mouth exposure, and have been published in some military newsletters.

Glossary

Acupressure A healing therapy in which finger pressure on the skin, rather than insertion of needles, is used to stimulate the acupuncture points.

Acupuncture An ancient Chinese therapy involving insertion of thin needles into the body at specific points in order to relieve pain or cure illness. Some conventional doctors now use acupuncture.

Allopathic medicine Conventional scientific medicine. This term was once used only by alternative practitioners in contrast to homeopathic medicine, but recently it has come into wider use.

Alternative medicine In its strict sense, whole systems of medicine used *in place of* conventional medicine. The term as used by the general public often includes complementary therapies.

Aromatherapy The use of fragrant oils extracted from herbs, flowers, and fruits to improve mood and promote healing.

Art therapy The use of creative activities such as painting or sculpture to express emotions and thereby promote psychological well-being.

Auricular acupuncture Acupuncture using only points found on the ears.

Ayurveda An alternative medical system emphasizing herbal remedies that has been practiced since ancient times in India.

Biofeedback A method of learning to control unconscious processes through real-time monitoring of specific aspects of the body's activity (such as heart rate and muscle action) with sensitive machines.

Botanicals Another term for herbal medicines.

CAM A widely used acronym for complementary and alternative medicine.

Chakra According to the theory of energy medicine and Eastern philosophies, a distribution center for chi corresponding to a specific point in the body.

Chelation therapy A controversial therapy that involves injecting a substance into the veins to bind with and thus remove traces of metallic elements such as lead and mercury.

Chi (pronounced "chee") An energy flow or life force unlike the energies known to science that, according to the theory of energy medicine and Eastern philosophies, permeates the bodies of living things. Illness is believed to be caused by an imbalance in the flow of chi.

Chiropractic An alternative medical system focused on manipulation of the spine that, according to its theory, can cure all types of diseases seemingly unrelated to the spinal column.

Codex Alimentarius Used as a noun in reference to the world trade guidelines that opponents fear might limit Americans' access to dietary supplements.

Colon hydrotherapy The process of flushing out the colon that some alternative practitioners believe is beneficial to health.

Complementary medicine Therapies that are not part of conventional medicine but are used along with it by patients who do not reject standard medical care.

Conventional medicine Scientific medicine as practiced by holders of medical doctor degrees. It is also known as Western medicine, since it is the standard form of health care in Western nations.

Crystal healing The use of crystals and gemstones to promote psychological and physical healing.

200

Dietary supplements Products taken by mouth—such as vitamins, minerals, herbs, amino acids, and enzymes—that are intended to supplement the diet. There is political controversy over whether the law should classify them as foods.

Dog therapy The use of specially trained service dogs to help people with physical or psychological disabilities.

DSHEA The Dietary Supplement Health and Education Act passed by Congress in 1994.

Energy medicine A collective term for therapies based on the concept of chi, such as acupuncture, qigong, Reiki, and therapeutic touch. The term is also used for therapies that employ measurable forms of energy, such as magnet therapy and light therapy.

Evidence-based medicine Medical treatment that has been formally verified by scientific tests.

Guided imagery Techniques used for visualizing an image in the mind to bring about a physical response, often employed for stress reduction.

Healing Touch (HT) A specific form of hands-on energy therapy similar to therapeutic touch.

Health freedom movement An informal coalition of organizations, activists, and consumers that seeks the same legal rights for CAM practitioners as exist for conventional practitioners and unrestricted access of the public to dietary supplements.

Herbal medicines Plants or parts of plants—such as flowers, seeds, leaves, and roots—used for therapeutic purposes.

Holistic medicine Medicine based on the philosophy that a patient should be viewed as a whole person—body, mind, and spirit—not just as a collection of symptoms or victim of a particular disease, and that treatment should address all three dimensions.

Homeopathy An alternative medical system based on the theory that disease can be successfully treated with minute doses of substances that in healthy people would produce symptoms of the disease.

Hypnotherapy The use of hypnosis to treat emotional or physical problems.

Integrative medicine Medical care in which both conventional medicine and complementary therapies are used. Some medical centers and hospitals, as well as individual physicians, now offer integrative medicine.

Iridology The analysis of patterns in the eye's iris that practitioners believe can locate areas of inflammation throughout the body and reveal many aspects of health.

Labyrinth walking Meditative walking along winding pathways laid out on the ground.

Massage therapy Rubbing or kneading the body's muscles and soft tissue to stimulate circulation and relieve stress or pain.

Medical acupuncture Acupuncture performed by a medical doctor or osteopathic physician rather than by someone trained in traditional Chinese methods.

Meditation Using a specific form of concentration or reflection to relax the body and calm the mind.

Meridian A channel undetectable by science through which, according to the theory of energy medicine, chi travels through the body.

Mind-body medicine Therapies that focus on the relationship between the brain, mind, and body with the aim of using the mind to promote physical health. Many forms of

CAM are of this type; however, the term is also used for conventional medicine that is based on research concerning the effects of the mind on the brain's biochemical control of the body.

Music therapy The use of music to promote emotional healing.

Naturopathy An alternative medical system based on belief in the curative power of nature and in the body's ability to self-heal that employs nutrition, herbal medicine, homeopathic remedies, and other healing therapies that do not involve drugs or surgery.

NCCAM The National Center for Complementary and Alternative Medicine, a US government agency run by the National Institutes of Health.

Neurofeedback A form of biofeedback in which brain activity is monitored by sensors placed on the scalp, often with the aim of learning to control the central nervous system.

Osteopathy A form of medicine based on the belief that most diseases are related to problems in the musculoskeletal system and that the body functions as a whole. Doctors of osteopathy (DOs) receive the same basic training as medical doctors and are legally allowed to prescribe drugs and perform surgery.

Placebo A drug or treatment that in itself is inactive, or is active in some way not relevant to the condition being treated. Placebos are commonly used for comparison purposes in drug testing.

Placebo effect Real improvement in the condition of a patient who was given a placebo but believes he or she received actual treatment.

Prana The term corresponding to chi used in India and in yoga.

Qi Another spelling of chi.

Qigong (sometimes spelled qi gong) A form of Chinese energy medicine in which breathing techniques, gentle movement, and meditation are used to strengthen and circulate life energy (chi/qi).

Quack A pretender of medical skill, properly applied only to fraudulent practitioners but often used pejoratively to refer to any practitioner whose methods are not based on established science.

Reflexology A therapy involving specific techniques for applying thumb or finger pressure to the feet or hands, based on the theory that zones on the feet and hands reflect an image of the whole body.

Reiki A form of energy medicine similar to therapeutic touch that originated in Japan.

Shiatsu A Japanese form of acupressure in which therapists use finger and palm pressure on the energetic pathways (meridians) of the body to improve the flow of chi.

Tai chi An ancient martial art now used to promote health that involves slow body movement and controlled breathing.

TCM A widely used acronym for traditional Chinese medicine.

Therapeutic touch (TT) A form of energy medicine developed by a registered nurse in which the practitioner's hands, lightly touching or near the body, manipulate energy fields in order to promote healing.

Traditional Chinese medicine (TCM) The medical system developed in ancient China and still widely used there today. It consists of acupuncture, other energy therapies, and herbal remedies.

Traditional medicine A term formerly used as a synonym for conventional medicine but now applied only to medical systems based on ancient traditions. In addition to TCM and Ayurveda, it can include healing techniques such as those traditionally employed in Africa and by Native Americans.

Yin and yang Opposing principles such as male/female, light/dark, dry/wet, and positive/negative. According to the philosophies on which Chinese medicine is based, such principles interact to create everything in the universe and must be balanced in the human body.

Yoga A form of non-aerobic exercise involving precise postures, derived from Hindu philosophy but often practiced for health purposes in the West.

Organizations to Contact

The editors have compiled the following list of organizations concerned with the issues debated in this book. The descriptions are derived from materials provided by the organizations. All have publications or information available for interested readers. The list was compiled on the date of publication of the present volume; names, addresses, phone and fax numbers, and e-mail and Internet addresses may change. Be aware that many organizations take several weeks or longer to respond to inquiries, so allow as much time as possible.

American Association of Acupuncture and Oriental Medicine (AAAOM)
PO Box 162340, Sacramento, CA   95816
(866) 455-7999 • fax: (916) 443-4766
e-mail: info@aaaomonline.org
website: www.aaaomonline.org

The American Association of Acupuncture and Oriental Medicine (AAAOM) is the national, professional association promoting and advancing high ethical, educational, and professional standards in the practice of acupuncture and Oriental medicine (AOM) in the United States. The organization's mission is to promote excellence and integrity in the professional practice of acupuncture and Oriental medicine to enhance public health and well-being. Its website contains past issues of its magazine, the *American Acupuncturist*.

American Association of Integrative Medicine (AAIM)
2750 East Sunshine, Springfield, MO   65804
(877) 718-3053 • fax: (417) 823-9959
website: www.aaimedicine.com

The mission of the American Association of Integrative Medicine (AAIM) is to promote the development of integrative medicine. AAIM focuses on the implementation and maintenance of successful credentialing programs and research that educate practitioners in the integration of safe and effective medical treatment modalities into health care. The organization publishes the *Journal of the American Association of Integrative Medicine (JAAIM)*, and archives are available at its website.

American Association of Naturopathic Physicians (AANP)
4435 Wisconsin Avenue NW, Suite 403
Washington, DC   20016
(866) 538-2267 • fax: (202) 237-8152
website: www.naturopathic.org

The American Association of Naturopathic Physicians (AANP) is the national, professional society representing licensed or licensable naturopathic physicians who are graduates of four-year, residential graduate programs. Its membership consists of more than two thousand students, physicians, and supporting and corporate members who collectively strive to expand access to naturopathic medicine nationwide. Its website contains general information about naturopathy and a directory of naturopathic physicians.

American Holistic Health Association (AHHA)
PO Box 17400, Anaheim, CA   92817
(714) 779-6152
e-mail: mail@ahha.org
website: www.ahha.org

The purpose of the American Holistic Health Association (AHHA) is to offer free and impartial information about health and wellness resources to the public, including both conventional and alternative medicine. The AHHA focuses on integration of mind, body, and spirit. The organization's website contains many self-help articles and videos, pro and con information about controversial issues, and a directory of resources.

American Holistic Medical Association (AHMA)
23366 Commerce Park, Suite 101B, Beachwood, Ohio 44122
(216) 292-6644 • fax: (216) 292-6688
e-mail: info@holisticmedicine.org
website: www.holisticmedicine.org

The American Holistic Medical Association (AHMA) serves as the leading advocate for the use of holistic and integrative medicine by all licensed health care providers. It embraces integrative, complementary, and alternative medicine (CAM) techniques while holding onto what is helpful in allopathic medicine. Its website contains frequently asked questions about CAM, a glossary of CAM therapies, and a newsletter archive.

American Institute of Homeopathy (AIH)
101 S. Whiting Street, Suite 16, Alexandria, Virginia 22304
(888) 445-9988
website: http://homeopathyusa.org

The American Institute of Homeopathy (AIH) is a trade association of medical and osteopathic physicians, dentists, advanced practice nurses, and physician assistants dedicated to the practice, promotion, and improvement of homeopathic medicine. The AIH emphasizes the dissemination of homeopathic medical knowledge through publishing, public speaking, and education. The organization's website contains information about evidence for the effectiveness of homeopathy. The AIH publication *American Journal of Homeopathic Medicine*, a peer-reviewed scientific journal, is not available online.

Committee for Skeptical Inquiry (CSI)
Box 703, Amherst, NY 14226
(716) 636-1425
website: www.csicop.org

The Committee for Skeptical Inquiry (CSI) is a nonprofit, scientific, and educational association. The mission of the CSI is to promote scientific inquiry, critical investigation, and the use of reason in examining controversial and extraordinary claims in many different fields. The organization publishes the magazine *Skeptical Inquirer*, the archives of which are available at its website.

National Center for Complementary and Alternative Medicine (NCCAM)
31 Center Drive, MSC 2182, Building 31, Room 2B-11
Bethesda, MD 20892-2182
website: http://nccam.nih.gov

The National Center for Complementary and Alternative Medicine (NCCAM) is a US government agency operated by the National Institutes of Health. NCCAM is dedicated to exploring complementary and alternative healing practices in the context of rigorous science, training complementary and alternative medicine (CAM) researchers, and disseminating authoritative information to the public and professionals. The agency's website contains detailed information on the major CAM therapies.

National Center for Homeopathy (NCH)
101 S. Whiting Street, Suite 315, Alexandria, VA 22304
(703) 548-7790 • fax: (703) 548-7792
e-mail: info@nationalcenterforhomeopathy.org
website: www.homeopathic.org

The National Center for Homeopathy (NCH) is an open-membership organization whose mission is to promote health through homeopathy. The NCH provides general education to the public about homeopathy, offers specific education to homeopaths, and works with government agencies and the media to make homeopathy understood and available throughout the United States. The organization's website contains articles about homeopathy for the public, but online access to its magazine *Homeopathy Today* is available only to members.

Bibliography

Books

Brent Bauer, ed.   *Mayo Clinic Book of Alternative Medicine*. 2nd ed. New York: Time Home Entertainment, 2010.

R. Barker Bausell   *Snake Oil Science: The Truth About Complementary and Alternative Medicine*. New York: Oxford University Press, 2009.

Roberta Bivins   *Alternative Medicine?: A History*. New York: Oxford University Press, 2007.

John R. Cross   *Acupuncture and the Chakra Energy System: Treating the Cause of Disease*. Berkeley, CA: North Atlantic Books, 2008.

Norma G. Cuellar   *Conversations in Complementary and Alternative Medicine*. Sudbury, MA: Jones & Bartlett, 2006.

Donna Eden   *Energy Medicine: Balancing Your Body's Energies for Optimal Health, Joy, and Vitality*. New York: Tarcher, 2008.

Edzard Ernst, ed.   *Healing, Hype, or Harm? A Critical Analysis of Complementary or Alternative Medicine*. Charlottesville, VA: Societas, 2008.

John S. Haller Jr. *The History of American Homeopathy: From Rational Medicine to Holistic Health Care.* New Brunswick, NJ: Rutgers University Press, 2009.

James M. Humber and Robert F. Almeder *Alternative Medicine and Ethics.* Totowa, NJ: Humana Press, 1998.

Bradly P. Jacobs and Katherine Gundling *The ACP Evidence-Based Guide to Complementary and Alternative Medicine.* Philadelphia, PA: American College of Physicians, 2009.

Richard A. Jaffe *Galileo's Lawyer: Courtroom Battles in Alternative Health, Complementary Medicine and Experimental Treatments.* Houston, TX: Thumbs Up Press, 2008.

Lucinda E. Jesson and Stacey A. Tovino *Complementary and Alternative Medicine and the Law.* Durham, NC: Carolina Academic Press, 2010.

Frank John Ninivaggi *Ayurveda: A Comprehensive Guide to Traditional Indian Medicine for the West.* Westport, CT: Praeger, 2008.

Ian N. Olver and Monica Robotin *Perspectives on Complementary and Alternative Medicine.* Hackensack, NJ: World Scientific Publishing, 2011.

Kenneth R. Pelletier *The Best Alternative Medicine: What Works? What Does Not?* New York: Simon & Schuster, 2007.

Rose Shapiro *Suckers: How Alternative Medicine Makes Fools of Us All.* London: Harvill Secker, 2008.

H. Robert
Silverstein

Maximum Healing: Optimize Your Natural Ability to Heal. Berkeley, CA: North Atlantic Books, 2010.

Simon Singh and
Edzard Ernst, eds.

Trick or Treatment: The Undeniable Facts About Alternative Medicine. New York: Norton, 2008.

Patricia Tsang

Optimal Healing: A Guide to Traditional Chinese Medicine. San Francisco, CA: Balance for Health Publishing, 2008.

Dana Ullman

The Homeopathic Revolution: Why Famous People and Cultural Heroes Choose Homeopathy. Berkeley, CA: North Atlantic Books, 2007.

Periodical and Internet Sources

Lesley Alderman

"Acupuncture Is Popular, but You'll Need to Pay," *New York Times*, May 7, 2010.

Lesley Alderman

"Using Hypnosis to Gain More Control over Your Illness," *New York Times*, April 15, 2011.

Dorian Ayers and
Jacob Swilling

"Pink: Fad or For Real?" Holistic Health Articles, November 28, 2010. www.holistichealtharticles.com.

William J. Broad

"Applying Science to Alternative Medicine," *New York Times*, September 30, 2008.

Benedict Carey   "When Trust in Doctors Erodes,
                      Other Treatments Fill the Void," *New
                      York Times*, February 3, 2006.

Abby Ellin   "Skin Deep: Ancient, but How Safe?"
                      New York Times, September 18, 2008.

Edzard Ernst   "Illusionists at Work," *Skeptical
                      Inquirer*, September/October 2010.

John Gever   "Hidden Dangers of Herbal Meds
                      Reviewed," Medpage Today, February
                      1, 2010. www.medpagetoday.com.

Harriet Hall   "The One True Cause of All Disease,"
                      Skeptical Inquirer, January/February
                      2010.

Samuel Homola   "Should Chiropractors Treat
                      Children?" *Skeptical Inquirer*,
                      September/October 2010.

Peter Jaret   "Awash in Ancient Hindu Wisdom,"
                      New York Times, March 9, 2006.

Kathi J. Kemper,   "The Use of Complementary and
Sunita Vohra, and   Alternative Medicine in Pediatrics,"
Richard Wells   *Pediatrics*, December 2008.

Jennifer A.   "Aromatherapy: Competing for Your
Kingson   Nose," *New York Times*, July 28, 2010.

Walecia Konrad   "Path to Alternative Therapies Is
                      Littered with Obstacles," *New York
                      Times*, November 13, 2009.

Alex Lickerman "Alternative Medicine Problems
Patients Need to Know About,"
KevinMD.com, March 2011.
www.kevinmd.com/blog.

George Lundberg "There Is No Alternative Medicine,
Only Unproven Medicine,"
KevinMD.com, September 2010.
www.kevinmd.com/blog.

Priyanka P. "Ayurveda's Struggle for a Level
Narain Field," Livemint, September 30 2010.
www.livemint.com.

Steven Novella "The Poor, Misunderstood Placebo,"
Skeptical Inquirer, November/
December 2010.

Shantanu Nundy "Allopathic Medicine Has Alternative
Medicine Roots," KevinMD.com,
March 2010. www.kevinmd.com/blog.

Meg Daley "Dog Good," *Psychology Today*, May
Olmert 5, 2010.

Tara Parker-Pope "Studying Acupuncture, One Needle
Prick at a Time," *New York Times*,
August 24, 2010.

Vinay Prasad "Toward a Meaningful Alternative
Medicine," *Hastings Center Report*,
March 11, 2010.

Len Saputo "Is It Time to Make Health Freedom
a Constitutional Right?"
NaturalNews, February 28, 2011.
www.naturalnews.com.

Science Daily   "Acupuncture Changes Brain's
                     Perception and Processing of Pain,
                     Researchers Find," November 30,
                     2010. www.sciencedaily.com.

Heidi Stevenson   "Study Proclaiming Dangers of
                     Alternative Medicine Is So Flawed It's
                     Useless," Gaia Health, December 26,
                     2010. www.gaia-health.com.

Abigail Zuger   "The Lure of Treatments Science Has
                     Dismissed," *New York Times*,
                     December 25, 2007.

Index

A

Acupressure massage, 70

Acupuncture, 19, 25, 26, 37, 40,
48, 67, 68, 75, 175
history, 67, 70–71
produces no greater effect
than placebo, 79–84
promotion, 59, 60, 69
rates of practice, 69, 71, 77–
78, 159
regulation, 62
safety, 76, 77
treatment described, 75–77
treatment purposes, 70–78,
80, 129

Adverse effects reporting, 150–151,
152

Advertising and marketing
dietary supplements, 59, 61,
64–65, 148–149
quackery, 55

Affordable Health Care Act
(2010), 128, 159–162

African medicine, 176

AIDS care, 72

Airborne, 64

Alcohol and drug abuse treatment
acupuncture, 72
art therapy, 192–193

Alexander technique, 27

Allopathic medicine. *See* Conventional medicine

Alternative medicine
legal status, 53–55

shouldn't be integrated with
conventional medicine,
35–45
terminology, 16, 23
See also Complementary and
alternative medicine (CAM)

Ama (Ayurvedic medicine), 107

American Art Therapy Association, 191

American Association of Naturopathic Physicians, 119–122

American Cancer Society
complementary therapy recommendations, 175–176
dietary supplements warnings,
177

American Heart Association data,
32

American Medical Association
(AMA)
acupuncture, 71, 77
history and power, 128–129

American Music Research Center,
185

American Music Therapy Association, 184, 186

Amygdalin, 125, 167

Angell, Marcia, 118

Angioplasty, 32–33

Anti-vaccination movement, 128,
135, 144–145

Aromatherapy, 37, 51, 53, 175

Arsenic, as medication ingredient,
59, 64, 109, 115–116

Art therapy, 19, 175, 183, 188–193

Arthritis treatments
acupuncture, 72, 78